# A WORLD FULL OF
# JOURNEYS & MIGRATIONS

Written by

## MARTIN HOWARD

Illustrated by

## CHRISTOPHER CORR

Frances Lincoln
Children's Books

# CONTENTS

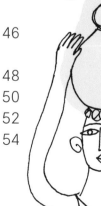

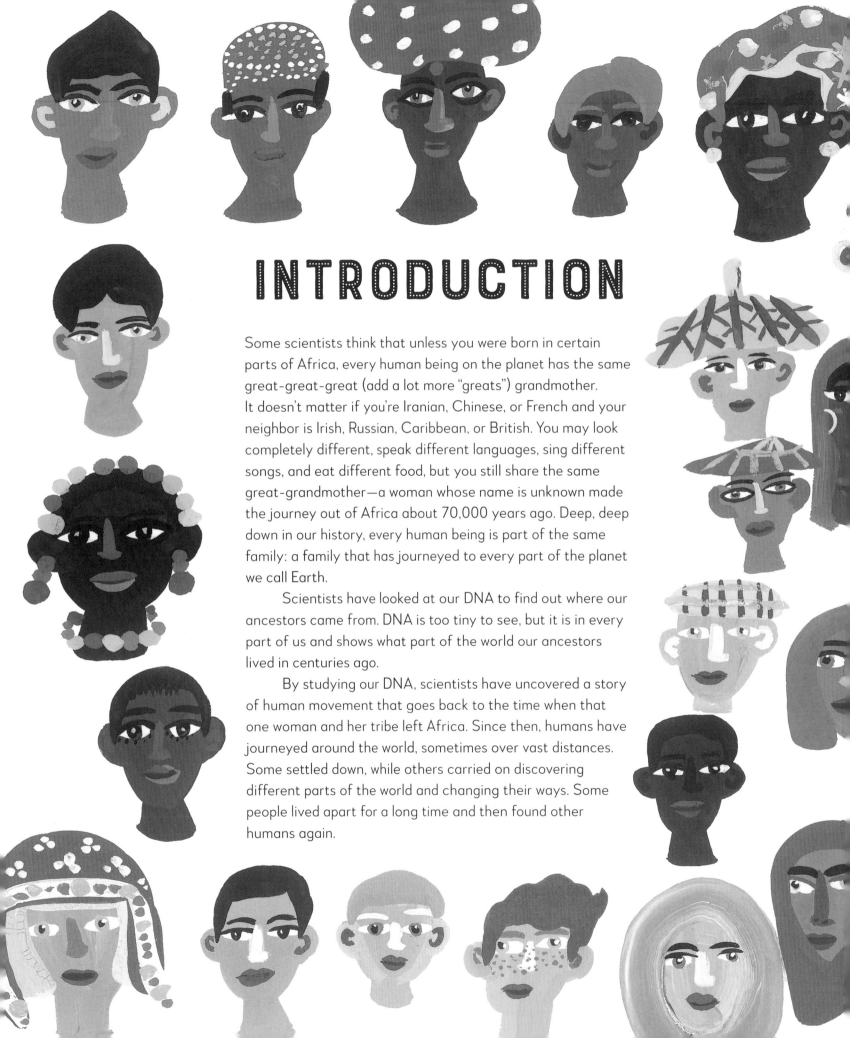

# INTRODUCTION

Some scientists think that unless you were born in certain parts of Africa, every human being on the planet has the same great-great-great (add a lot more "greats") grandmother. It doesn't matter if you're Iranian, Chinese, or French and your neighbor is Irish, Russian, Caribbean, or British. You may look completely different, speak different languages, sing different songs, and eat different food, but you still share the same great-grandmother—a woman whose name is unknown made the journey out of Africa about 70,000 years ago. Deep, deep down in our history, every human being is part of the same family: a family that has journeyed to every part of the planet we call Earth.

Scientists have looked at our DNA to find out where our ancestors came from. DNA is too tiny to see, but it is in every part of us and shows what part of the world our ancestors lived in centuries ago.

By studying our DNA, scientists have uncovered a story of human movement that goes back to the time when that one woman and her tribe left Africa. Since then, humans have journeyed around the world, sometimes over vast distances. Some settled down, while others carried on discovering different parts of the world and changing their ways. Some people lived apart for a long time and then found other humans again.

They mingled with each other, had babies, learned their neighbors' languages, told stories, and played music. They swapped ideas that created exciting new ideas. They learned from each other, changing again and again down the years. And then they moved on once more in a slow, never-ending journey around the globe that still goes on today.

Inside you is a kaleidoscope of human history, and thousands of stories of travel and adventure. In this book we are going to discover over 50 of those stories. So what are you waiting for? Let's get ready to uncover a world full of journeys.

CLIMATE CHANGE

# WHY WE MOVE

Some people in history never traveled further than the next village. Others made long and difficult journeys into the unknown, facing danger along the way. Below are just some of the reasons why people moved.

Changes in the Earth's climate are nothing new! Some of our ancestors were forced to move away from green and fertile lands because they turned into deserts.

TRADE

Merchants and traders took long journeys over land and sea to swap or sell goods such as wool or furs, metal for jewelry and weapons, and spices for food.

## SEARCH FOR FOOD

In ancient times there were no farms or stores selling food. Everything our ancestors ate, they found themselves. Most early humans were always on the move, following animal trails so they could hunt meat or looking for new places to pick plants and berries.

Some people made journeys for adventure and discovery. When they found new lands the settlers who followed often caused terrible problems for people already living there.

Across history, bad rulers made peoples' lives miserable. Armies invaded towns and villages, destroying farms and taking prisoners. Even today, people leave their homes to find more peaceful lives.

WAR

War brings terror and destruction, but it also brings new settlers. Throughout history, armies arrived with people who stayed in the conquered lands, changing the laws, languages, stories, clothes, food, and ideas.

The San people of southern Africa still live similar lives to their distant hunter-gatherer ancestors. In 2012, a set of tools was discovered in a cave. They were almost exactly the same as those used by the San today, but were 44,000 years old!

# THE FIRST JOURNEYS

Even before our earliest ancestors evolved into humans, they knew how to make musical noises with their voices and clap their hands to make rhythms. Hunter-gatherers improved their musical skills by making drums and other instruments.

About 70,000 years ago a small tribe of human beings walked out of Africa and into the country we now call Yemen in the Middle East. With them was the woman who would become the grandmother to all humans outside of Africa. Others had made the journey before them, but eventually they all died out. But this group was different. They were true humans—or homo sapiens, to give the scientific name—just like us. They survived and spread, and slowly their numbers increased. Today, there are over seven billion of us, living in every corner of the world.

Our distant ancestors were called hunter-gatherers. They discovered fire, danced, made stone tools and musical instruments, and were always on the move—looking for animals to hunt or different foods to forage. At first, they stayed close to the ocean, making simple raft-boats so they could catch fish. Some sailed from island to island until they reached a new continent—Australia. Later, people made even longer ocean voyages, finding their way by following the stars and reaching new homes on islands scattered across the oceans.

Other humans began to journey inland, to what we now call China and Russia and westward into Europe. They invented the needle so they could sew warm clothes and live in colder places. More time passed and finally, around 20,000 years ago, humans discovered a thin strip of land that allowed them to walk from Russia into a brand-new continent—America. Humans had discovered another vast new home.

Some scientists believe that our ancestors ate a better diet than we do today! They hunted meat and foraged vegetables, fruits, nuts, and berries.

9

EUROPE

ASIA

AFRICA

OCEANIA

AUSTRALIA

AUSTRALASIA

**MIGRATION** OF **MODERN HUMANS**

NORTH AMERICA

PACIFIC OCEAN

SOUTH
AMERICA

Many people around the world share the same old stories. One of the most famous is the tale of a great flood that swept across the Earth. This ancient story can be found all around the world, from Norway to China, to South America.

12

# THE FIRST STORYTELLERS

No one knows exactly when humans first used language to talk to each other. However, historians believe that as soon as humans began using language, they probably started telling stories: grand tales of great hunts, exciting deeds of their ancestors, and terrible natural disasters. They may have told stories of gods and goddesses and the sun, moon, and stars.

Stories traveled as humans moved from place to place. They were told and retold, changing and developing as they passed from mouth to mouth, from tribe to tribe, translated into different languages. Humans became a species that loved stories and today, thousands of years later, we still do.

The first story ever written down was called the *Epic of Gilgamesh*. It tells the tale of a mythical king and was written more than 4,000 years ago, though the story is probably a lot older. Writing stories down meant they could be told again and again. As this new invention spread, people wrote poems and plays, stories, and histories.

Now, we can watch movies or television and read books. But the art of storytelling began thousands of years ago when our ancestors sat around crackling fires, listening to stories that still travel from one end of the Earth to another.

Ancient people sometimes painted their stories onto rock walls. Some of the earliest cave-paintings are in Lascaux, France, and are about 17,000 years old. The people who made them chose to paint pictures of hunting— a very important part of their lives.

13

# A WORLD OF
# MUSIC AND DANCE

Everywhere the first hunter-gatherers traveled, they left evidence of their love of music—ancient flutes made from mammoth tusks or animal bones, or didgeridoos, horns, drums, and rattles. Today, there is nowhere in the human world that doesn't have music and dancing. From the largest nations to the smallest tribes, people play songs and dance. This probably means that our most ancient ancestors in Africa loved music and dancing, too. And, like their stories, the songs of ancient humans spread from place to place and down through generations.

Over time, different groups of people invented new instruments, and new kinds of music, which could mix to make completely new sounds. For example, fast and thrilling Spanish flamenco dance music is thought to have developed from very, very old Spanish music that was mixed with the music of those who made new homes in Spain, including ancient Greeks, Romans, and North African people.

14

Dancing is as old as music and early humans probably used it as a way of communicating before they could even talk! Among the oldest clues we have are simple cave paintings in India that date back 30,000 years.

The first instrument with strings was a lyre. It was invented more than 6,500 years ago. Over thousands of years its design slowly changed, making different sounds until the guitar was invented around 600 years ago.

For thousands of years humans have been swapping flavors. Tea came from India and China, spices from Southeast Asia, while fruits from South America and India made long journeys to tables in Europe and beyond.

16

# FOOD, GLORIOUS FOOD

In English, "turkeys" are named so because new arrivals in America mistook them for a bird that they thought came from the country of Turkey. In French they're called "dinde" or "d'inde," which means "from India."

Humans started farming and settled down in towns and cities about 12,000 years ago. Traders made long journeys selling spices such as cinnamon, pepper, and ginger, which made bland dishes taste better. Food was traveling as well as humans!

Plants, too, began traveling around the world with merchants and explorers. The globe-trotting journey of the chilli pepper is just one example of this. We now think of fiery curries, flavored with red-hot chilli, as being a food of India, but there were no chilli peppers in India before 1498. They were brought to the country from South America by an explorer called Vasco da Gama. When the British ruled India in the 19th century, they took hot curries back home. Chillis made another long journey and curries became part of British culture.

Whether you're sprinkling sugar from Brazil on your cornflakes, eating chocolate from Africa, or drinking tea from India, what you eat and drink may have taken a long journey to end up in your mouth!

Potatoes arrived in Britain from America with the explorer Sir Walter Raleigh when Elizabeth I was queen. At first, many people thought they were supposed to eat the green, leafy parts of the plant and throw away the potatoes!

# AFRICA

Africa is a vast and beautiful continent full of color, history, and wonder. It is also where the story of humans begins; the place where our ancestors evolved from apes and invented the first tools and musical instruments.

The first true humans, called homo sapiens, were born in Africa around 300,000 years ago and slowly spread over the continent. About 70,000 years ago the woman, who some scientists around the world today call Eve (after the first woman God created in *the Bible*), left Africa with her small tribe. This was the beginning of the great human journey around the world.

Tens of thousands of years after Eve had been forgotten, people from other lands returned to Africa. They had invented new languages, new clothes, new stories, and new foods and had no idea that the people living in Africa were their cousins. Some came to trade, while others came to conquer. Africa had fertile lands, amazing wildlife, precious metals, and jewels. All too often these riches—even Africa's people—were stolen.

Africa has fifty-four countries, each with its own heritage and culture; from Egypt with its history of great pyramids and powerful pharaohs, to the rolling grasslands of Botswana. Here, the cultures of our most distant ancestors can still be found today, as well as sleek, modern skyscrapers. With its incredible landscapes, astonishing wildlife, and amazing history, Africa is the continent where the human story began.

Over centuries people became better at farming and inventing new tools. That meant even more food could be grown. More food fed more people and so the number of people grew and grew.

20

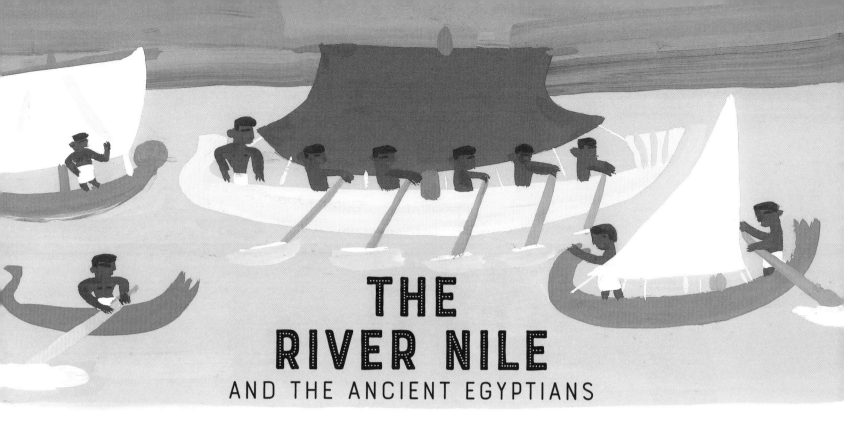

# THE RIVER NILE
## AND THE ANCIENT EGYPTIANS

On the fertile River Nile, more food meant more free time. Some folk invented new jobs, including making pottery or leather goods, or making jewelry from gold and precious stones. People now made new journeys, to trade with other people.

Around 12,000 years ago the Sahara Desert dried out and the people who lived there were forced to find new homes when their green lands turned to sand. This early example of climate change led them to settle on the River Nile, in the land we now call Egypt. Instead of hunting and gathering food the first Egyptians began growing crops and raising animals.

Farming completely changed the way people lived. Instead of constantly moving in search of food they could stay in one place. Some people became unimaginably wealthy—especially the kings and queens, or "pharaohs" as they were called. They spent their riches on fantastic temples, vast monuments, and great tombs such as the pyramids at Giza.

Many people around the world have moved because of climate change. Long ago, tribes in South America abandoned their homes when lakes dried up. People in Greenland moved when ice covered their lands. Hunter-gatherers changed migration routes to find food when woodland turned to grass.

The markets of Carthage sold many wonderful things. The city was famous for its cloth, especially one of rich purple, which was dyed with a color that came from the murex shellfish.

# AFRICA'S SHOPKEEPERS

In ancient times, Africa's great wealth attracted merchants and traders with an eye for profit. Almost 3,000 years ago, in 814 BCE, a group of people from Phoenicia on the eastern shores of the Mediterranean Sea decided to move to Africa permanently. The Phoenicians built a small colony—a town called Carthage—in the country now called Tunisia. It was in an excellent position to trade for jewels, gold, and other metals with the Africans and to ship these goods to other cities around the Mediterranean. Carthage grew and a great harbor was built, filled with ships. They would have seen strange goods arriving from distant lands, and heard many different languages. Sailors from Carthage even traveled as far north as the cold island of Britain.

Carthage owed its success to its two great harbors, which were wonders of engineering. Hundreds of ships from around the Mediterranean and further away came here to unload their cargoes.

The Phoenician people who built Carthage chose the site of their new city well. Its huge harbors were bustling places where goods from around the known world were bought and sold.

Nomadic people have lived across North Africa for thousands of years. Many build homes but some continue the nomadic lifestyle of their ancestors, moving their goats and camels to areas in the Sahara Desert where fresh grazing can be found.

# THE NOMADS OF AFRICA

The word "nomad" means "without a home" and there are millions of people in Africa (and around the rest of the world) who travel endlessly. Nomads never stay in one place for very long. They take everything they own with them when they move and live in tents or portable shelters as they follow herds of cattle, goats, or camels in search of grazing land, often in places where grass and water is scarce. Their lives are very much like the lives of our most distant ancestors. They make their own clothes—some in dizzying colors—paint their bodies, and perform traditional songs and dances. Often they hunt for food with birds of prey, and forage for their meals, living side by side with nature.

Nomadic people were important because they moved trade goods across the desert. They remembered places where water and grass for their animals could be found by weaving them into their songs and stories.

25

# EUROPEANS IN AFRICA

More than 12 million African people—men, women, and children—were shipped across the Atlantic Ocean, and sold into slavery around the world.

When people travel, amazing things can happen. We learn new songs and discover different ideas from each other, even if it's something as simple as a delicious new recipe. When we journey in peace, humans come together, and the world becomes a better place.

Sadly, not all of history's great journeys have been peaceful. Thousands of years after humans left Africa, their descendants began coming back, conquering the people who lived there and taking the land and its treasures for their own. In 1652, the first European town was built by the Dutch at the bottom tip of Africa, in the country we now call South Africa. Over the next three centuries, more arrivals came in tall sailing ships from all over Europe—Britain, France, Spain, Italy, Belgium, Germany, and Portugal. They came with modern weapons and took almost everything from the Africans who had lived there for thousands of years. By 1914, almost all of Africa was ruled by European countries.

Today, the age of Europeans invading Africa is over, but those difficult years have left many scars in Africa's history. Slowly, those scars are healing, and Africa is making a new journey—a journey to peace and prosperity.

One of the few places that remained free was Ethiopia. Its emperor, Menelik II, successfully brought together the people and tribes of his country to fight off invasion.

In the 19th century, European settlers poured into the continent, determined to claim Africa's wealth for their own. Africa was rich in resources such as diamonds, gold, rubber, and timber.

An Apartheid law, known as the "Pass Law," made it illegal for Black people to be in a white-only area without permission. Black people could be arrested for walking in the wrong part of their own country!

Apartheid is pronounced "apart-hide." In the Afrikaans language of South Africa, which was used by Dutch settlers, it means "segregation" or "apartness."

28

# DIVIDED SOUTH AFRICA

Nelson Mandela (below) began protesting against white-only rule of South Africa in 1943 and was sent to prison in 1962. By the 1980s, millions of people around the world were demanding his release, and huge music concerts were held to shout the message *"Free Nelson Mandela."*

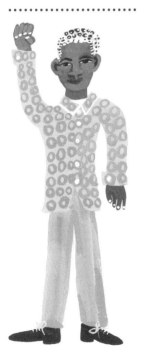

Across the 19th century, large groups of Europeans settled in countries across Africa. The effects of this could be seen in South Africa in the 20th century—Black people were forced apart from the white community under a system of laws known as "Apartheid." In 1949, the first Apartheid law made marriage between a white and Black person illegal. Neighborhoods were divided into Black-and white-only areas—a Black person could be arrested for something as simple as strolling in the wrong part of town. Black people couldn't vote, white schools wouldn't accept Black children, and their parents couldn't get the well-paid jobs that were only for white people. Apartheid was viciously enforced and protests against these racist laws were brutally squashed.

This oppressive system lasted until the early 1990s. By then, the rest of the world had become outraged at Apartheid. Meanwhile, the voices of Black people in the country were growing louder. They demanded change and the release of protesters from prisons.

Nelson Mandela, a Black South African, was imprisoned in 1962 for fighting for his peoples' rights. In 1990, after spending 27 years in jail, he was released and four years later was elected as the country's first Black president. Apartheid was finally over, but today South Africa still suffers from the terrible division it caused. Black citizens in South Africa are still far more likely to live in poverty than their white neighbors.

When Mandela was released from prison in 1990, he worked alongside the country's president, F. W. de Klerk (below), to make sure that in the future South Africa would be a fairer place. The two men were awarded the Nobel Peace Prize for their efforts.

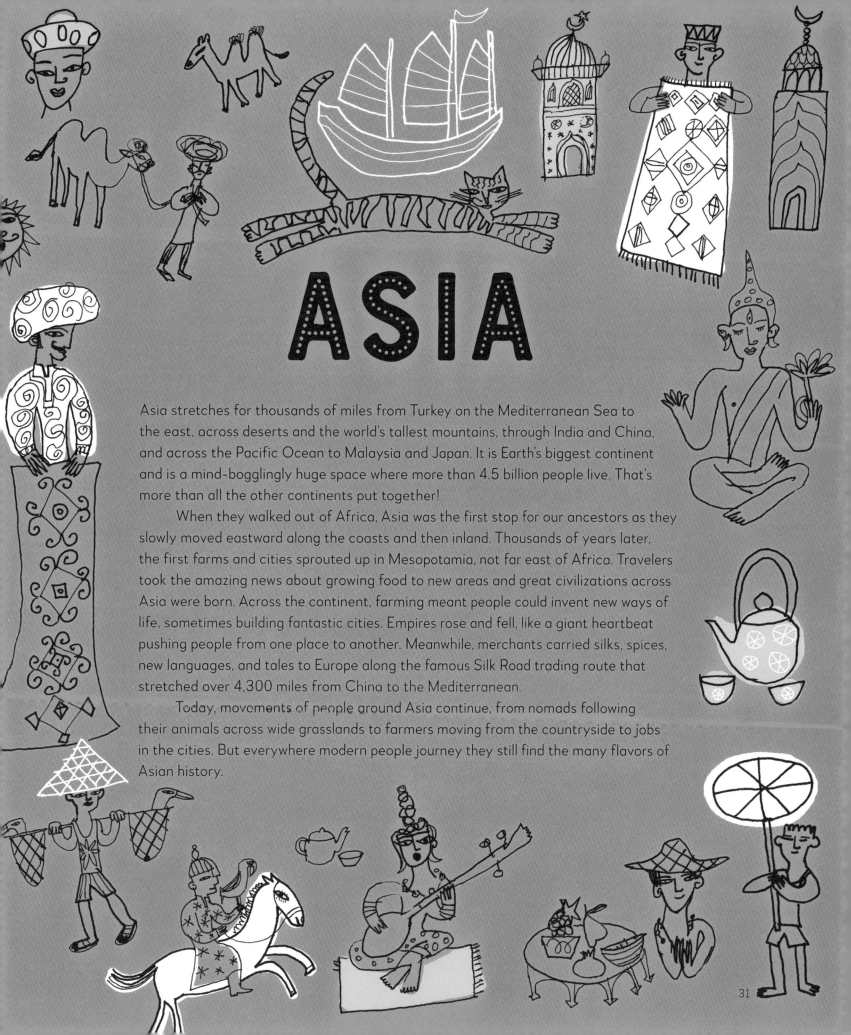

# ASIA

Asia stretches for thousands of miles from Turkey on the Mediterranean Sea to the east, across deserts and the world's tallest mountains, through India and China, and across the Pacific Ocean to Malaysia and Japan. It is Earth's biggest continent and is a mind-bogglingly huge space where more than 4.5 billion people live. That's more than all the other continents put together!

When they walked out of Africa, Asia was the first stop for our ancestors as they slowly moved eastward along the coasts and then inland. Thousands of years later, the first farms and cities sprouted up in Mesopotamia, not far east of Africa. Travelers took the amazing news about growing food to new areas and great civilizations across Asia were born. Across the continent, farming meant people could invent new ways of life, sometimes building fantastic cities. Empires rose and fell, like a giant heartbeat pushing people from one place to another. Meanwhile, merchants carried silks, spices, new languages, and tales to Europe along the famous Silk Road trading route that stretched over 4,300 miles from China to the Mediterranean.

Today, movements of people around Asia continue, from nomads following their animals across wide grasslands to farmers moving from the countryside to jobs in the cities. But everywhere modern people journey they still find the many flavors of Asian history.

As king, Alexander arranged marriages for hundreds of his soldiers to Persian women. He wanted to bring Macedonia and Persia closer together and raise children with the heritage of both civilizations.

32

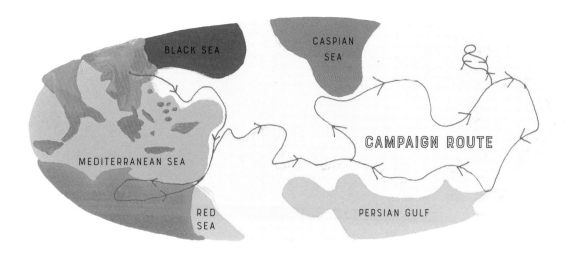

BLACK SEA

CASPIAN SEA

MEDITERRANEAN SEA

CAMPAIGN ROUTE

RED SEA

PERSIAN GULF

# ALEXANDER THE GREAT

In 336 BCE, Alexander the Great was just 20 years old when he became king of Macedonia—a small country north of Greece. He was young for a king and even younger for a mighty conqueror, but he was unstoppable. With a small army, he marched on mighty Persia, destroying cities that stood against him, and sparing those that welcomed him. By the time his long march across Asia came to an end, he had become the richest man in the world, the Persian King of Kings, and the ruler of a vast empire.

On foot or horseback, Alexander's army journeyed thousands of miles, from the Mediterranean Sea and across wide grasslands, sandy deserts, and rocky mountains. Along the way he built new cities and brought the Greek way of life to the East. A child born during Alexander's long march eastward might have seen the world change around her. She would have begun hearing Greek stories as well as Persian tales, listened to Greek music for the first time, and seen new buildings rising with Greek columns and carvings. Meanwhile, Alexander's soldiers took the ways of the East back to Europe, including the Persian love of gardens, and stories of their gods. Alexander himself loved wearing rich Persian silks!

Alexandria in Egypt was a city built by Alexander. It became one of history's most amazing places, with an incredible lighthouse and the biggest library on Earth. Two and a half thousand years later, it is still a bustling city.

# ASHOKA
## AND THE SPREAD OF BUDDHISM

Around 268 BCE, almost 2,300 years ago, a king was crowned in India. He was a violent man called Ashoka who loved conquering new lands. Eventually, his empire covered almost all of India. But despite all this, he is not remembered as a conqueror but as a man who spread peace.

Eight years after he came to the throne, Ashoka sent his army to conquer the land of Kalinga in the east of India. It was a terrible war that cost more than 100,000 lives and many more people were forced from their homes. Horrified by the terrible suffering he caused, Ashoka gave up violence forever and instead turned to Buddhism, a way of life that teaches its followers to find inner peace through quiet meditation, always showing kindness and compassion for others.

For the rest of his reign, Ashoka spread Buddhist teachings far and wide. He lived a life of peace, loved by his people, and built hospitals and temples. He toured around his empire preaching peace, and sent monks to distant countries. His works helped Buddhist teachings eventually reach almost every part of Asia. Thousands of years later, the effects of the work Ashoka started can still be seen. Great Buddhist temples are scattered across Asia and millions of people across the continent still follow the peaceful teachings of Buddha.

Today, hundreds of millions of people around the world follow the teachings of Buddhism—peace, generosity, and kindness toward others.

Wherever Buddhism spread, people built amazing temples as well as huge statues of the Buddha. The largest is the 233-foot-tall Leshan Giant Buddha in Sichuan, China.

It is said that Ashoka sent groups of monks to teach the world about Buddhism. One group crossed the Himalayan Mountains, another crossed the ocean to Sri Lanka and another traveled to Thailand. Others traveled far and wide across India.

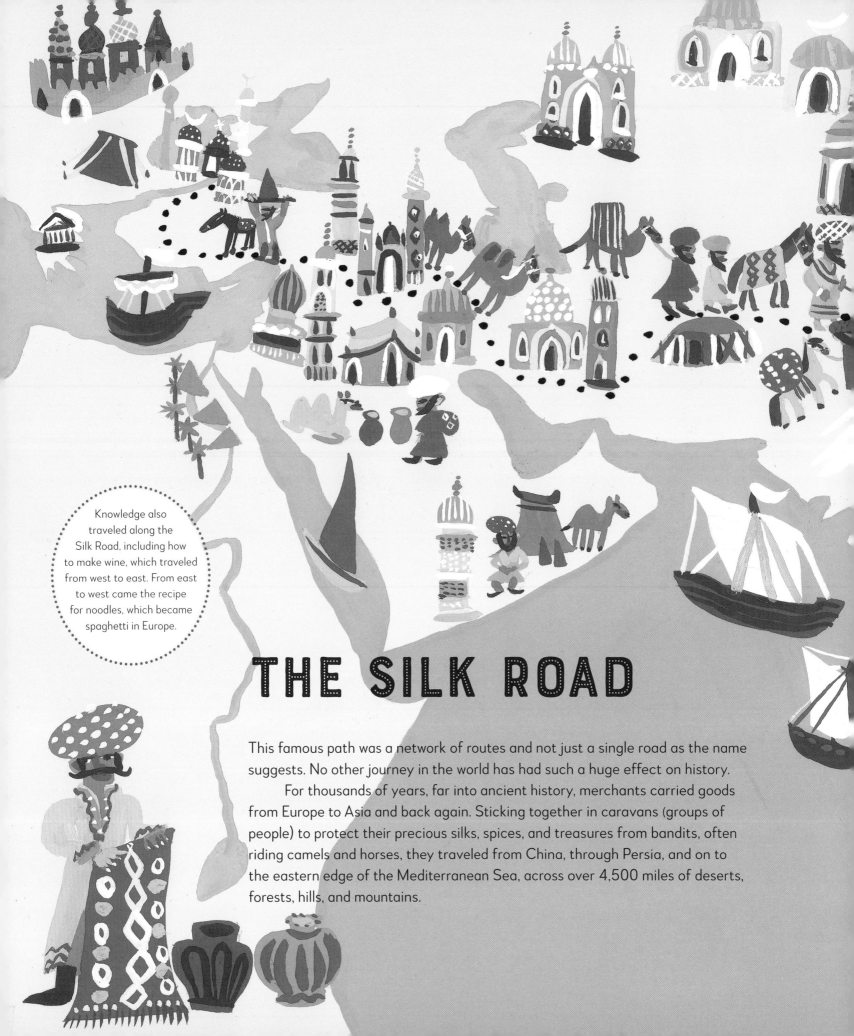

Knowledge also traveled along the Silk Road, including how to make wine, which traveled from west to east. From east to west came the recipe for noodles, which became spaghetti in Europe.

# THE SILK ROAD

This famous path was a network of routes and not just a single road as the name suggests. No other journey in the world has had such a huge effect on history.

For thousands of years, far into ancient history, merchants carried goods from Europe to Asia and back again. Sticking together in caravans (groups of people) to protect their precious silks, spices, and treasures from bandits, often riding camels and horses, they traveled from China, through Persia, and on to the eastern edge of the Mediterranean Sea, across over 4,500 miles of deserts, forests, hills, and mountains.

A journey along the Silk Road led through spectacular landscapes and amazing cities like Petra, an entire city carved into red cliffs, and Xi'an, the site of the biggest royal palace ever built.

No one knows when merchants began traveling between Europe and Asia, but silk fragments found in the tombs of Egyptian royalty tell us that Silk Road trade may have begun around 10,000 years ago!

The journey along the Silk Road took an entire year by horse or camel. Sleeping under the stars, or stopping at inns, merchants making the trip from the Mediterranean to China and back were away from home for at least two uncomfortable and dangerous years.

Huge profits from silk, which was only made in China (because the method of how to make it was secret), and other goods made the journey worthwhile but languages, stories, and new technologies—such as the printing press and gunpowder—traveled with the traders, too. The long road meant people at opposite ends of Asia learned from each other, beginning a process we call 'globalisation' today.

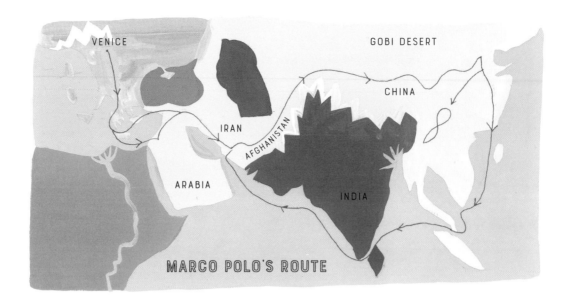

MARCO POLO'S ROUTE

# THE JOURNEY OF
# MARCO POLO

Marco Polo's long journey made a huge circle around Asia, from Persia to the far shores of China, down through the country that is now Vietnam and around India. No one from Europe had seen so much of Asia before.

In 1271, almost 800 years ago, a young man named Marco Polo set off on an amazing journey from his home in Venice to China. It lasted 24 years, during which he saw more of Asia than anyone had ever seen before.

He was not the first European to travel along the Silk Road to China, but his adventures were astonishing. He met the great emperor Kublai Khan—lord of what's known as the greatest empire the world had ever seen—and journeyed to many parts of China on the Emperor's business.

When he returned, Marco went to sea, commanding a ship in a war against the Republic of Genoa. He was captured by the enemy and put in prison where he told his story to his cellmate, Rustichello da Pisa. Da Pisa added some fantastic details from his own imagination and wrote a book, called *The Travels of Marco Polo*. It caused a sensation! Marco Polo's story was translated into many languages and gave the people of medieval Europe their first glimpse of fabulous, faraway India, China, and Japan. For the first time, people across Europe began to understand that amazingly different ways of life existed in distant parts of the world.

Marco Polo helped people in medieval Europe understand how big the world was. For the first time, they could read of steamy jungles and forests of bamboo, or travel across the great empty sands of the Gobi Desert.

# THE BRITISH IN INDIA

Born in India in 1869, Gandhi trained as a lawyer in London, England, before returning to India. A peaceful man, he campaigned to end British rule without bloodshed. Today, he is often remembered as Mahatma Gandhi ("Mahatma" means "great soul") and many think of him as the father of modern India.

In the 19th century, Britain was at the center of an empire that stretched around the globe. In 1858, the British conquered India. A small number of British officials and soldiers governed a huge country of more than 300 million people during a time known as the British Raj ("Raj" means "rule").

Very few of the new arrivals were interested in Indian traditions and the British wanted India to become as much like home as possible. They used Indian people as cheap workers who did almost everything for them—many became servants and others became soldiers and were sent to fight British wars. Back in India, the British forced Indian farmers to grow new crops such as tea and cotton, which they could sell for huge profits. This meant there wasn't enough food for poorer Indians, and many starved.

In the early 20th century Indian leaders began demanding an end to British rule. Led by a lawyer called Mohandas Karamchand Gandhi (often known as Mahatma Gandhi), Indian people across the country started to disobey British laws and took part in peaceful protests.

Gandhi eventually led his people to freedom and the British finally left India in 1947. By then it had become a very different place to the country it had once been and, today, reminders of British rule still mark India. Today, India is part of the British Commonwealth, a group of nations that were once part of the British Empire, and the two countries are at peace with each other.

During the Raj, British life took root in India. Churches, libraries, schools, gardens, and clubs were built until some parts of India looked just like Britain. Under British command, Indian workers built India's railway system, which is still used today.

# THE HIPPIE TRAIL

Among the thousands of young people who took the Hippie Trail to India were the four members of the Beatles—the most famous pop band in the world during the 1960s.

Back in the 1960s many young people called themselves "hippies." They grew their hair long, wore groovy, colorful clothes with beads and flowers and went looking for peace and love.

Their search led them to India, where they found peaceful religions, sunshine, and freedom. Following the route of the old Silk Road, thousands of hippies hitch-hiked or drove thousands of miles from European countries through places such as Turkey, Iran, and Afghanistan, where ancient traders once rode camels and Alexander the Great's armies had marched. They traveled through lands that had been untouched by the modern world for years. The clothes, rock music, and Western ways of the new visitors were so strange to the locals that they were often left confused! Many of these travelers had little money, but they shared information with each other and many cheap hotels and restaurants along the route became popular as a result.

In India, the hippie travelers often talked to the local people. The Indians taught them about Buddhism—with its vegetarian diet and love of animals—as well as meditation and yoga. Some hippies spent years soaking up Indian religion and culture, sharing what they learned when they finally returned. Journeys along the Hippie Trail are partly the reason why yoga and meditation classes are now popular in Europe and America.

Hippies used trains, cars, and buses to travel thousands of miles to India. The brightly painted "psychedelic" trucks they had decorated were often seen along the route.

JOHN

PAUL

GEORGE

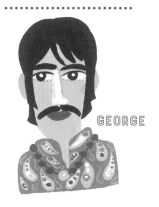

RINGO

The visitors heard people playing amazing instruments, including the guitar-like sitar, and saw colorful, exciting festivals. Along the sacred River Ganges, Indian Hindus floated flowers and lamps and bathed in the holy waters.

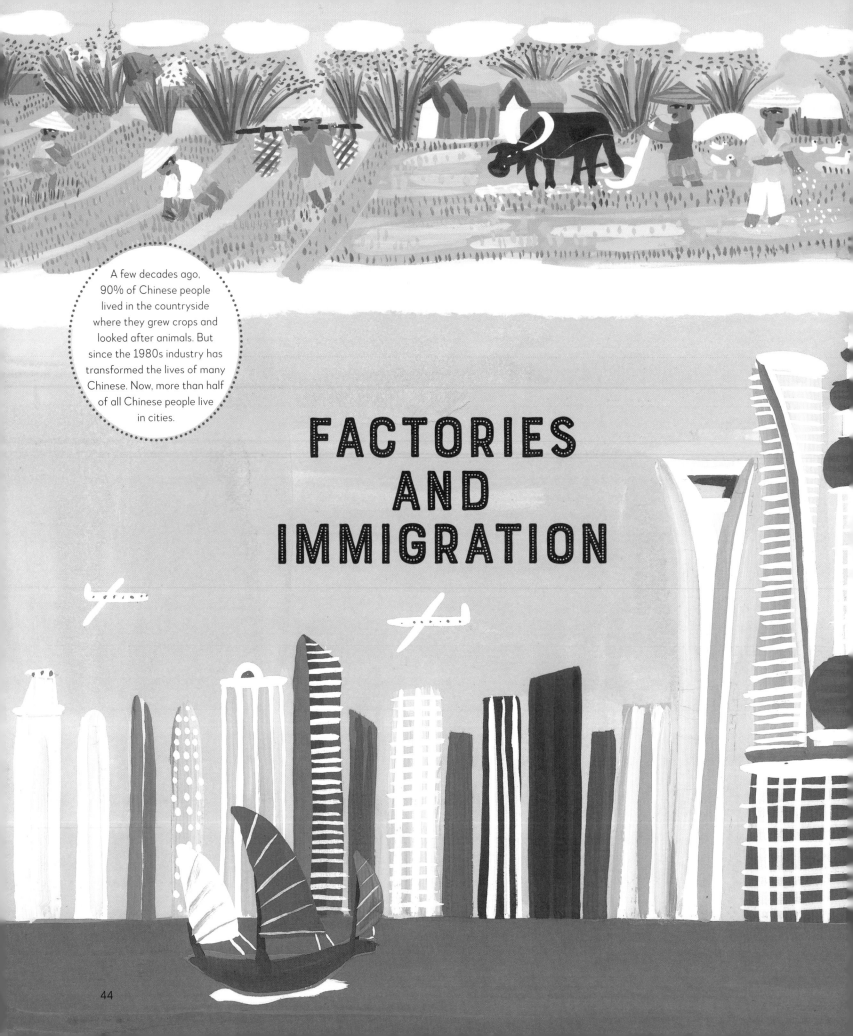

A few decades ago, 90% of Chinese people lived in the countryside where they grew crops and looked after animals. But since the 1980s industry has transformed the lives of many Chinese. Now, more than half of all Chinese people live in cities.

# FACTORIES AND IMMIGRATION

Almost 300 years ago, a great change swept across the world as steam engines sparked the Industrial Revolution into life. Landscapes transformed as massive factories packed with new machines were built. Cities grew as people moved from their old jobs in the countryside to earn money in the new industries. It is a process that still goes on today—especially in China.

A few decades ago, China was a country of farmers. Most of its people lived the same lives as their ancestors, raising crops and looking after their animals in small villages. But now, China is the biggest industrial country in the world. Hundreds of millions of people have moved away into the cities— the greatest, and fastest, movement of people history has ever seen.

Like everywhere in the world that has seen great migrations of people to the cities, many changes have taken place. Today's Chinese people can expect better standards of living than their grandparents, including better schools and healthcare. However, their cities are often overcrowded, with lots of traffic on the roads, and plumes of harmful pollution.

It is interesting to compare the new Chinese mega-cities to cities in the West, where many factories have disappeared. Now, more and more people in the West are moving back to smaller towns and villages outside the cities. Connected by the internet, they no longer need to be gathered in one great city.

In the past 30 years, Chinese cities have grown upward as more people moved in. Places like Beijing, Shanghai, and Chongqing are now bristling with enormous tower blocks and skyscrapers.

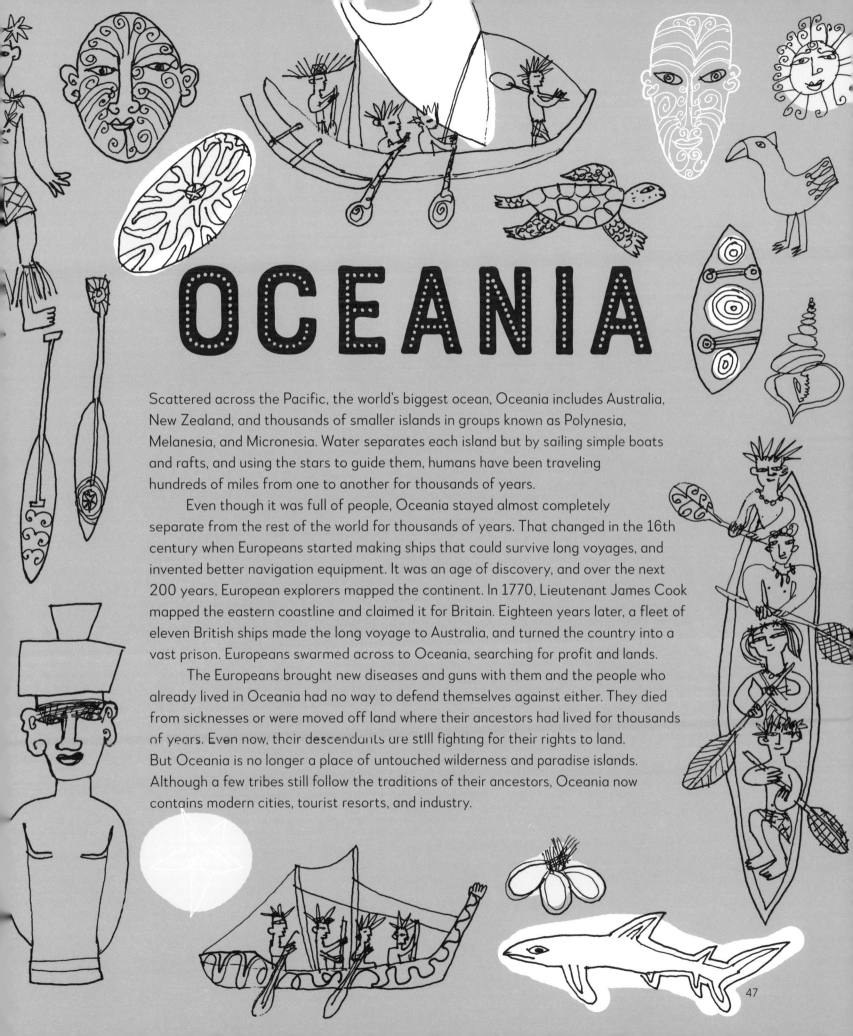

# OCEANIA

Scattered across the Pacific, the world's biggest ocean, Oceania includes Australia, New Zealand, and thousands of smaller islands in groups known as Polynesia, Melanesia, and Micronesia. Water separates each island but by sailing simple boats and rafts, and using the stars to guide them, humans have been traveling hundreds of miles from one to another for thousands of years.

Even though it was full of people, Oceania stayed almost completely separate from the rest of the world for thousands of years. That changed in the 16th century when Europeans started making ships that could survive long voyages, and invented better navigation equipment. It was an age of discovery, and over the next 200 years, European explorers mapped the continent. In 1770, Lieutenant James Cook mapped the eastern coastline and claimed it for Britain. Eighteen years later, a fleet of eleven British ships made the long voyage to Australia, and turned the country into a vast prison. Europeans swarmed across to Oceania, searching for profit and lands.

The Europeans brought new diseases and guns with them and the people who already lived in Oceania had no way to defend themselves against either. They died from sicknesses or were moved off land where their ancestors had lived for thousands of years. Even now, their descendants are still fighting for their rights to land. But Oceania is no longer a place of untouched wilderness and paradise islands. Although a few tribes still follow the traditions of their ancestors, Oceania now contains modern cities, tourist resorts, and industry.

47

Aboriginal people did not invent writing but expressed themselves in amazing rock paintings and told stories. These tales were passed from generation to generation across thousands of years.

# FINDING AUSTRALIA

Aboriginal people made music with many instruments and sang songs about the Dreaming—a time when giant ancestors with supernatural powers walked the land.

Because Australia is a long way away to travel by ocean from Africa, you might think that it took a long time for our simple hunter-gatherer ancestors all those thousands of years ago to get there. After all, they didn't have proper boats or navigation equipment! But, in fact, humans made it all the way to Australia about 65,000 years ago, which is 25,000 years before they even started living in Europe—and it would have been a lot closer to go there!

Back then, ocean levels were lower than they are today. This meant that more land was above water, and meant our ancestors could hop from Asia to Australia, island by island, under the blazing sun or through tropical storms, with only the stars as a guide. Those first explorers wouldn't have known if any new lands lay across the distant horizons. Theirs was an incredible journey of seafaring skill and courage and they discovered an untouched world populated by strange plants and animals.

In the centuries after these ancient folk first made their home in Australia, Earth's ocean levels slowly rose. The Australian hunter-gatherers, or the Aboriginal people of Australia as they are known, were almost completely cut off from the rest of the world and developed their own way of life, undisturbed by outsiders for tens of thousands of years.

The land is sacred to Aboriginal people, especially places connected to the Dreaming. They marked these sites with paintings and monuments, like the mysterious stone circle at Mullumbimby.

The group of 300 islands we now call Fiji were discovered up to 5,500 years ago. Fijiian stories tell of a canoe arriving with the first king—Lutunasobasoba—who built large sailing boats and beautiful buildings.

# POPULATING THE
# SOUTH SEAS ISLANDS

Between 7,000 and 5,000 years ago, people from the islands north of Australia—such as Papua New Guinea and Indonesia—began sailing longer distances. There were many reasons to make such dangerous voyages across hundreds of miles of empty ocean. Some might have been escaping wars between tribes, while others simply enjoyed the thrill of adventure and exploration.

The Pitcairn Islands were discovered 1,000 years ago and for the next 400 years people flourished there. But food became harder to find and people began fighting. Eventually people left the Pitcairn Islands and now, few people live there.

One important reason they traveled is because islands are small, and they only have room and food for a smaller number of people. When a population became too large, people went hungry. Many ancient South Seas explorers were probably looking for untouched islands with plenty of food... and they found many! Over thousands of years they made new homes across the Pacific Ocean and some even reached the shores of America.

EASTER ISLAND

NEW ZEALAND

People often think that the Māori people of New Zealand are as ancient as the Aboriginal peoples of Australia. However, seafaring explorers actually only reached the islands of New Zealand around 700 years ago.

Easter Island is one of the world's most remote islands. Even so, ancient sailors discovered this speck of land in a vast ocean around 800 years ago. The island's people carved hundreds of giant stone heads called moai.

# THE VOYAGE OF **THE *KON-TIKI***

At the beginning of the 20th century, researchers didn't understand how ancient people had reached tiny islands in the middle of the Pacific Ocean. Sailing such long distances on simple rafts or canoes seemed impossible. However, in 1947 a Norwegian man named Thor Heyerdahl put their questions to the test when he proved it could be done.

He believed that people from South America had settled on Easter Island, so he took a small crew to Peru and built a raft. Called the *Kon-Tiki* after a South American god, it was nearly 46 feet long and 18 feet wide. It had a bamboo and banana leaf hut where the crew could shelter, and a square sail.

Even though the *Kon-Tiki* carried a radio, its journey was very dangerous. The craft was all alone, hundreds of miles from land. If Heyerdahl and his crew got into trouble, there was little chance anyone would have been close enough to help.

Thor Heyerdahl had never built a boat before, was not a sailor, and couldn't even swim! Ancient people who were experts at building boats and rafts and navigating by the stars might safely have traveled longer distances than the *Kon-Tiki*.

Heyerdahl wanted to find out how far such a primitive vessel could sail so, carrying just a few modern supplies such as a radio for safety, the *Kon-Tiki* set sail from Peru on April 28, 1947. Over the next 101 days it journeyed eastward. The crew caught fish, drank water from bamboo containers, and ate fruit and vegetables they had brought with them. Finally, the *Kon-Tiki* hit a reef on the Tuamoto Islands. The great journey was over, and the little raft had voyaged 4,500 miles, proving that, with a brave crew, sailing vast distances on simple boats could be done.

This amazing voyage inspired others to find out how far ancient sailors might have traveled. Others have sailed longer distances across the Pacific Ocean, while a raft called the *An-Tiki* made a nearly 3,000-mile trip across the Atlantic in 2011.

# AUSTRALIA'S NEW ARRIVALS

It wasn't just people who arrived with the First Fleet. The eleven ships carried everything the prisoners needed to start a colony, including farm tools, seeds, cows, sheep, horses, and even rabbits. The European rabbits spread faster than humans and today there are billions in Australia!

In 1770, when the British explorer and mapmaker James Cook landed in a natural harbor he named Botony Bay (now in the city of Sydney), he wasn't the first European to discover Australia. However, he was the first to suggest that the continent would be a good place for settlers. At that time, even small crimes such as stealing a loaf of bread meant harsh punishment and Britain's prisons were overflowing. To make sure that they could continue to house all of these prisoners it was decided that Australia would become a "penal colony;" in other words, a huge, outdoor prison.

After zig-zagging across the Atlantic Ocean, facing storms, disease, and hunger, the eleven ships of the First Fleet arrived in Botany Bay in 1788, bring more than 1,000 prisoners to their new home. Amazingly, only forty-eight people died during the 250-day journey.

At first, life was hard and fighting soon broke out with the Aboriginal people when it became clear the British had arrived not as new friends, but as the masters of Australia and everything it contained. Soon after the First Fleet arrived, people began exploring the vast new continent. The government also started giving away land so cheaply that it was almost free! Vast areas of Australia where the Aboriginal peoples had roamed freely now belonged to Europeans and, by 1815, it wasn't only prisoners making the long voyage to Australia. Others came, too, looking for a new life on the other side of the world. Over the next 100 years, Britain sent more and more people to Australia, especially after gold was discovered. Australia was no longer just a prison colony—it was a land where fortunes could be made!

Few Europeans thought about the people already living in Australia. Their arrival caused much suffering for the Aboriginal peoples. Lands where they had lived for thousands of years—and sacred sites—were taken from them.

European diseases spread like wildfire. Attempts to defend their lands were met with violence and gunfire. More than 250 years later, the Aboriginal people of Australia are still fighting for their rights.

# EUROPE

True humans—homo sapiens—first made the journey to Europe around 40,000 years ago, much later than they reached Australia. They faced three problems on their arrival. First, it was cold! Ice covered a lot of Europe and humans had to learn how to make and use needles to sew clothes before they could live there. Secondly, hunting was more difficult: the animals were larger and special skills were needed to capture them. Thirdly, there were already people living there: not human beings as we know them today but Neanderthals, the descendants of even earlier humans.

But our ancestors were fast and clever and, over about 20,000 years, they spread across Europe. Eventually, the Neanderthals died out, though not before having a few babies with their human cousins. Even today, many Europeans have a little Neanderthal DNA in them!

As the ice melted, more people arrived from the East. Over centuries, Europeans often fought each other, but they also swapped ideas, inventions, and even DNA. Eventually people settled into the different countries we know today. In more recent times, its people journeyed to faraway lands such as America and Australia, while others arrived from all over the world.

Today, Europe has an amazing history and a huge mix of people. More are still coming, for work or to escape war and poverty. With so many different people, Europe is now a colorful patchwork where it is possible to hear different languages spoken on the same street, and smell food or hear music from across the globe.

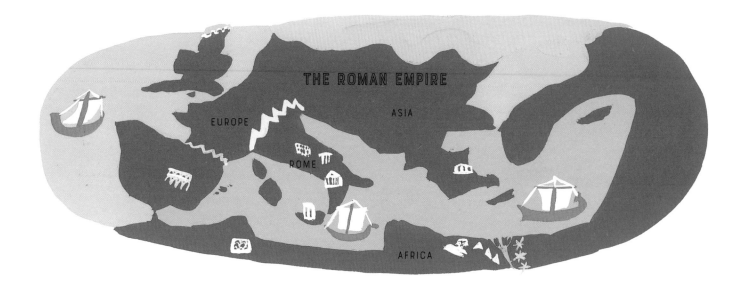

# ROMAN EUROPE

Around 3,000 years ago a small tribe of people in Italy changed the world. They called themselves the Romans after their home city of Rome, and eventually ruled almost all of Europe along with large parts of Asia and Africa.

The Romans were masters of engineering and building, and were amazingly well-organized. Rome's great armies marched, unstoppable, across the known world, conquering every culture that stood in their path and bringing almost all of Europe together under one rule for the first—and only—time in history. People who had been living in simple houses built from mud and wood watched as roads, great stone buildings, bath houses, and even theaters were built. Under Rome, Europe experienced a new era where people, ideas, art, music, and culture moved around like never before.

However, Roman rule wasn't without its share of drawbacks. Slavery came with these changes and many people were forced from their homes to serve their new Roman masters.

The great Roman Empire collapsed in Europe more than 1,600 years ago but it left Europe and the world changed forever. Ideas that had started in ancient Rome would be spread around the globe for centuries to come. Many are still part of our everyday life.

When the Roman Empire stretched from Europe to Asia and North Africa, African soldiers in the Roman army would have been sent as far north as Britain.

Wherever the Roman army conquered, people were sent to Rome to be slaves. This meant people from all over the Roman world—from Britain to Africa and the Middle East—could be found in Rome, where they were treated as property.

European travelers took Roman ideas, architectural styles, engineering, and laws to new places, like the Americas and Australia, spreading them around the globe.

# THE VIKING AGE

Vikings are often seen as bloodthirsty pirates, plundering their way across Europe after the Roman Empire crumbled. It's true that they were fierce people who loved grabbing whatever treasure they could find, but the Vikings were also traders, artists, and amazingly adventurous folk with their own laws and way of life.

From the 8th century to the end of the 11th century, they sailed sleek longboats across the oceans, using advanced navigational skills to explore the world from their Scandinavian homeland—today's Sweden, Norway, and Denmark.

The typical Viking longships were astonishing boats. They were long, graceful, and had both a sail and oars so they could always move. These ships could sail across the Atlantic Ocean but were light enough to be carried across land when needed.

The Vikings' fierce reputation was well-earned. They were sailor-warriors who would go a long way to steal valuables. Viking raids from Scandinavia reached as far south as Seville in Spain and Pisa in Italy.

They settled in places as far away as Russia, Greenland, and even the Americas, centuries before Christopher Columbus arrived there, and visited places far south, including the city of Baghdad in Arabia.

The Vikings loved gold and silver and brought great riches from their explorations back to their homeland. They also brought back new ideas that eventually put a stop to their endless plundering. Over time, the frightening warriors became more peaceful as the religion of Christianity spread. The Vikings' bloody raids stopped but they left their mark everywhere they had visited: beautiful art and thrilling stories of gods such as Thor and Loki that are still told today as well as their amazing seafaring knowledge. Centuries after the Viking Age had ended, their longboats were still copied by ship designers.

Although the Vikings were raiders, they also built towns that are busy cities today. Places such as York in England and Dublin in Ireland have Viking roots. Greenland and the Americas also had Viking settlements.

The Roma people have many different names across Europe. In Germany they are called Zigeuner and Sinti; in France, Gitans; and in Spain they are known as Gitanos. Today, some still ride in bright wagons but most use modern trucks and caravans.

# NEVER STOP TRAVELING

Most journeys eventually come to an end, and some even change the world. However, the travels of the people known as the Roma, or Romany, aren't like those journeys. These folk have been traveling for more than 1,000 years, never settling anywhere for long.

It is believed the Roma people first came to Europe from the north of India and ever since they have been moving from one place to another. In the past, they traveled with brightly colored wagons, pulled by horses, making money where they could as musicians, storytellers, and entertainers, or by fixing pans or trading horses. Some worked as vets. It has often been a difficult journey—many other people have tried to stop their travels or even force them out of the country.

Yet all attempts to stop the Roma people and their journey have failed. Despite hardships and suspicion and even violence against them, the Roma people carry on. Today, they can be found everywhere in the world, telling their own stories and changing the world in small ways. Today, different groups of Roma people still come together every year as they have done for centuries. One example is the Appleby Horse Fair, which takes place in Cumbria, England. Every year more than 10,000 Roma people come together from across Britain and Europe to trade, show off their horses, and enjoy a huge party.

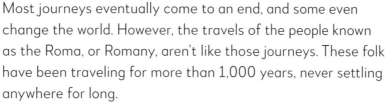

In the past, the Roma people used their love of music and dancing to make money. Many entertained towns and villages they passed through with their songs and stories. Spanish Flamenco dancing and its thrilling guitar music is thought to have been invented by Roma musicians and dancers.

# THE FIRST REFUGEES

History is full of stories of people fleeing violence and oppression, going all the way back to the most ancient times, but the Huguenots were the first to be called "refugees." The word comes from an old French word—refuge—which means to hide or shelter in a time of danger. Since then, it has been used to describe anyone trying to escape oppression.

In the 16th century the Catholic Church was very powerful across Europe but many Christians believed that people should be free to worship God as they liked, without being Catholic. In France, these people took the name Huguenots and by the end of the 16th century there were more than two million of them.

The Catholic Church did not agree with this outlook and made the Huguenots suffer for their beliefs. Torture and persecution became common and by 1572 the Huguenots knew they could no longer remain in France and secretly began leaving. They went to places where they could worship as they liked: places such as England, America, and the Netherlands. Over the next century, hundreds of thousands of Huguenots deserted France. This kind of journey is sometimes called a "brain drain." The reason behind this name is because the Huguenots were often well-educated or had useful skills. Wherever the Huguenots made their new homes, those countries became richer while France lagged behind. As Britain, America, and the Netherlands grew more successful with the help of their new Huguenot citizens, France grew poorer, suffering for its own intolerance. Even today, the story of the Huguenots has a lesson to teach us: societies that welcome new arrivals and make use of their skills and unique talents are always happier and more successful than places where new arrivals are unwelcome.

Around 50,000 Huguenots journeyed to Britain where they often settled into small communities around the country. They opened new businesses and transformed their new home towns with stores and businesses. Many places in Britain still have French street names thanks to the Huguenots.

The Huguenots had many skills in business, engineering, science, medicine, architecture, printing books, furniture making, glassblowing, and many more. They were also famous for their weaving skills, especially with silk.

QUEEN HATSHEPSUT

ALEXANDER VON HUMBOLDT

One of the first people known to send explorers to find new plants was the Ancient Egyptian queen Hatshepsut. She lived 3,500 years ago and sent ships to bring new trees and plants back to Egypt.

# SPREADING ROOTS

For thousands of years humans have found tasty, valuable, and beautiful plants on their travels and brought them back home, but in 18th-century Europe a craze for plant collecting started. Explorers and plant experts traveled to every corner of the world, often braving unmapped lands looking to collect or study rare and wonderful plants. Some people spent fortunes on unusual new species! Some of those species took root in Europe, growing far from their original soil and changing European gardens forever.

MARIANNE NORTH

JOSEPH DALTON HOOKER

Marianne North had a passion for exotic plants and flowers and braved many dangers, traveling the world to paint as many as possible. Back home in England, people were fascinated by her paintings.

Joseph Dalton Hooker visited the Antarctic, New Zealand, India, Africa, and the United States in search of new and unusual plants. He wrote a number of books and brought home many samples from his travels.

From 1799 to 1804, the German explorer Alexander von Humboldt traveled through wild parts of North and South America, making scientific observations and collecting thousands of plants.

JOHAN NIEUHOF

During the 17th century, Johan Nieuhof traveled across China, Brazil, and India and drew pictures of beautiful plants never before seen in Europe. This helped to start a fashion for plants from distant places.

There have been brick and tile works in Brick Lane since the time Queen Elizabeth I ruled England. However, the street first became home to new settlers from overseas in the 18th century, when Huguenots arrived from France. For decades, Brick Lane became a French-speaking center of cloth weaving and fashion. In 1743, its new residents also built a church on the corner of Fournier Street. The church was a simple brown building (seen behind the young boy's head in this picture) and would go through as many changes as Brick Lane itself over the following centuries.

# THE STORY OF
# BRICK LANE

Britain is built on waves of new arrivals. For thousands of years different people from near and far have helped make it a country with an amazing mix of cultures, languages, art, music, and food. The history of those people is often written into the streets where they settled, and sometimes into a single building. One such building on Brick Lane in East London is a great example of how each group of immigrants changed their new home to help suit their needs—it is also a symbol of how people working together in peace can help each other.

Like the Huguenots, many of Brick Lane's Jewish residents eventually moved out. The next wave of new people were Bengalis escaping war between Pakistan and Bangladesh in the 1970s. Many are still there today, and Brick Lane's latest arrivals have given the street the flavors of their home country with Islamic street art and curry houses. However, traces of its older residents still remain, including Jewish stores that sell the most amazing bagels! The Huguenot church that became a Jewish synagogue has changed again and is now a mosque used by Brick Lane's Muslim people.

BENGALIS ON BRICK LANE

ARTIST CENTRAL

As the Industrial Revolution began, the Huguenots were settled in their new country. Many left Brick Lane to find new homes in more leafy areas, and in the late 19th century the street welcomed a new group of residents. Jewish people fleeing oppression and violence in Eastern Europe and Russia soon made themselves at home on Brick Lane, and Jewish deep-fried cooking methods introduced Britain to fish and chips for the first time! Meanwhile, the church the Huguenots had built turned into a synagogue where Brick Lane's Jewish folk could practice their faith.

Today, Brick Lane has attracted yet another wave of new arrivals. With its rich history of welcoming outsiders it has become a destination for students, artists, and fashionable young people. Places where Huguenots once sewed expensive clothes might now be used again as fashion boutiques, and stores that once sold Jewish delicacies now sell vegan cupcakes and bubble tea. There is still a strong Bengali community too, and Brick Lane's many curry houses are famous, attracting diners from all over the city.

69

# THE KINDERTRANSPORT

Some of the children who joined the Kindertransport are still alive today. They often tell stories of their parents joking and waving them off at the station, saying that they were going on an adventure. It would be the last time they ever saw each other.

War and oppression always cause terrible grief and suffering, forcing adults and children from their homes. However, they can also bring out the best in humanity: this story is a perfect example.

In 1938, just before World War II, Nazis led by Adolf Hitler forced Jewish people into concentration camps where millions would be murdered. The world was horrified, and in Britain people did what they could to help. Across the nation, people came together to bring Jewish children across Nazi Germany, Austria, and Czechoslovakia to safety in Britain. Without any adults to help them, 10,000 Jewish children traveled on special trains called "Kindertransport." Packed trains and eventually ferries carried the scared, homesick children to Britain where people took them into their homes.

Jewish children were given clothes, food, and new homes. Some lived in special camps, but most were sent into foster families. Few of them ever saw their own parents again. The last of the Kindertransport trains left Germany on September 1, 1939, the day World War II began. After that, it became impossible to bring any more Jewish children to safety. Even though they had little more than the clothes they were wearing, the Kindertransport children were the lucky ones.

Little support for the Jewish children came from the government. Their lives were saved by individuals who opened up their homes and hearts to them and by different charities that also helped where they could. Today, this is a reminder that all of us can help when others are suffering.

Children of the Kindertransport often arrived at Liverpool Street Station in London. Today, there is a statue outside the station to commemorate their arrival and the warm hearts that helped these children escape the Nazi horrors.

The children had to
leave in a hurry. With nothing
but clothes and a few belongings,
hundreds boarded trains and
made the long journey to Britain.
Anything valuable they had was
often stolen by Nazis
along the journey.

The arrival of the *Empire Windrush* at the port of Tilbury, near London, marked the first time that immigrants from the West Indies had come to live and work in Britain. News cameras rolled as they walked off the ship.

Among those first arrivals were people who would make a big difference to society, such as Sam Beaver King. He became the first West Indian Mayor of Southwark, in London, and he founded the city's Notting Hill Carnival, which is still held every year.

EMPIRE WINDRUSH
LONDON

# THE WINDRUSH GENERATION

In the 1950s many companies refused to employ people of the Windrush Generation, but they found jobs in the National Health Service (NHS) and British Transport. Britain's much-loved NHS was partly built by the efforts of people from the Caribbean.

World War II left a lot of Britain in pieces. Nazi bombs reduced thousands of buildings to rubble, and many soldiers never returned home from the fighting. Britain needed new people to help rebuild it and advertised jobs overseas in countries that were still part of the British Empire, such as the Caribbean islands of Jamaica, Trinidad, and Bermuda, known as the West Indies.

The people there—who were the descendants of slaves brought from Africa—had fought alongside British troops during World War II. Many decided to take the long journey overseas to Britain, seeking jobs with good pay and new lives for their families. In 1948, 802 Caribbean people boarded a ship and sailed across the Atlantic Ocean to their new home. The ship would give its name to an entire generation of new arrivals in Britain. It was called the *Empire Windrush*.

But those who arrived didn't find the welcome they expected. Many companies refused to employ Black people and housing was difficult to find. Children were bullied because of the color of their skin. In some cities riots against the new arrivals broke out on the street.

Even so, the people who came to help rebuild Britain stayed and, over time, tens of thousands more joined them. Over the next decade or so, almost 200,000 people arrived from the Caribbean and, despite the racism they faced, they made their own mark on Britain. Their incredible hard work has helped create the vibrant culture we can see across the UK today.

Even today, people can be made to feel unwelcome in their home country. In 2018, the UK government began sending people of the Windrush Generation to the Caribbean, saying that they didn't have permission to be in the country! The scandal caused outrage and rocked the Government.

It's difficult to imagine life without tea or coffee, but before the 17th century neither drink was known in Europe. Early in the 1600s tea arrived in Portugal from China. Coffee was introduced by traders who brought in goods from Africa.

# A WORLD OF FOOD

Since traders first set out on long journeys thousands of years ago, they have carried food around the globe. Until then, people mostly ate whatever could be hunted or grown close by, so the arrival of a merchant carrying tasty spices, candies, and delicacies from distant lands must have been exciting for our ancestors. Over the years many people have become used to stores full of foods from distant shores but there are many places where traders still sell unusual spices and treats prepared in traditional ways.

TURKISH MARKET BERLIN, GERMANY

In Berlin's Turkish market, you'll find foods such as stuffed pastries called Gözleme and spicy stews as well as Turkish handicrafts. The market has become a much-loved part of the local culture and is very popular with tourists, too.

BRIXTON MARKET LONDON, ENGLAND

When West Indian people settled in Brixton, London, in the mid-20th century, its local market began selling food from around the world. West Indian foods like yams, plantains, and green bananas are especially popular today.

Since ancient times, Marseille in France has been a trading hub for goods coming from everywhere around the Mediterranean, especially North Africa. The amazing market here still exists today.

NORTH AFRICAN MARKET
MARSEILLE, FRANCE

75

# THE AMERICAS

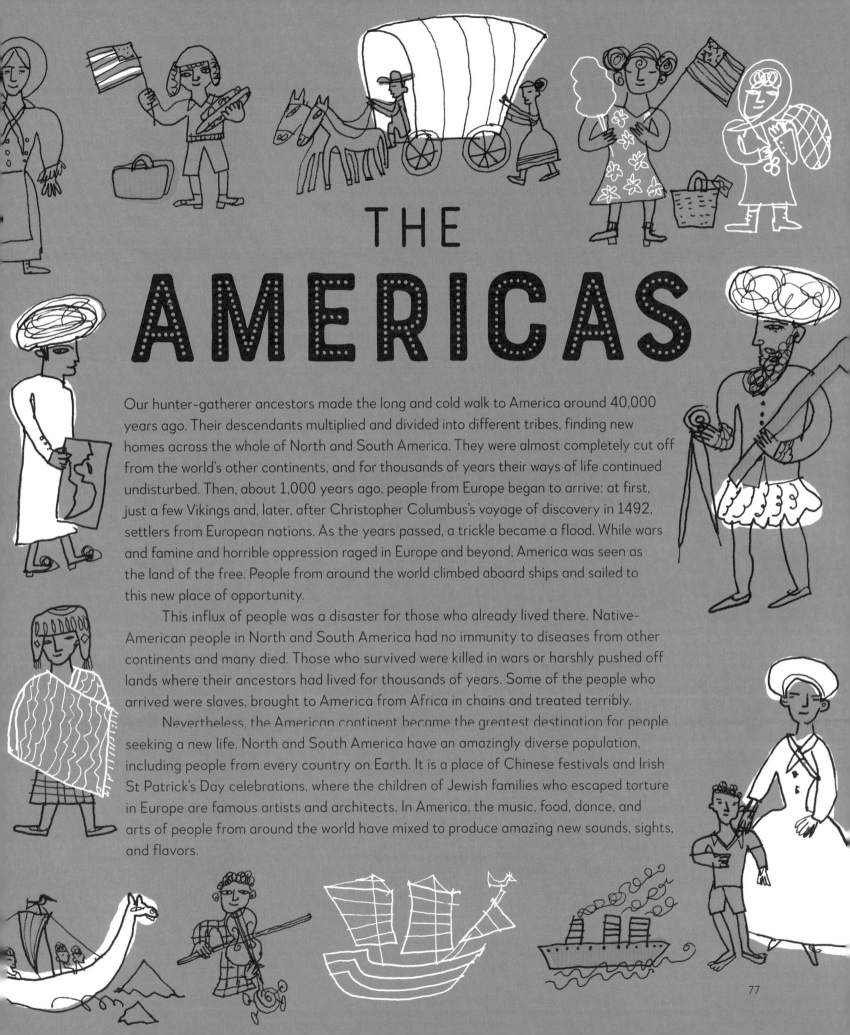

Our hunter-gatherer ancestors made the long and cold walk to America around 40,000 years ago. Their descendants multiplied and divided into different tribes, finding new homes across the whole of North and South America. They were almost completely cut off from the world's other continents, and for thousands of years their ways of life continued undisturbed. Then, about 1,000 years ago, people from Europe began to arrive: at first, just a few Vikings and, later, after Christopher Columbus's voyage of discovery in 1492, settlers from European nations. As the years passed, a trickle became a flood. While wars and famine and horrible oppression raged in Europe and beyond, America was seen as the land of the free. People from around the world climbed aboard ships and sailed to this new place of opportunity.

This influx of people was a disaster for those who already lived there. Native-American people in North and South America had no immunity to diseases from other continents and many died. Those who survived were killed in wars or harshly pushed off lands where their ancestors had lived for thousands of years. Some of the people who arrived were slaves, brought to America from Africa in chains and treated terribly.

Nevertheless, the American continent became the greatest destination for people seeking a new life. North and South America have an amazingly diverse population, including people from every country on Earth. It is a place of Chinese festivals and Irish St Patrick's Day celebrations, where the children of Jewish families who escaped torture in Europe are famous artists and architects. In America, the music, food, dance, and arts of people from around the world have mixed to produce amazing new sounds, sights, and flavors.

ARCTIC OCEAN

BERINGIA LAND BRIDGE

PACIFIC OCEAN

# THE FIRST AMERICANS

Around 40,000 years ago, it was possible to walk from Russia, across cold, northern lands where giant mammoths roamed, into the vast continent we now call North America. At the time, the oceans were lower than they are today, and a narrow strip called the Beringia Land Bridge connected Russia to what is now the American state of Alaska. This strip of land was eventually covered by rising ocean levels but over thousands of years the hunter-gatherer people traveled to every corner of North and South America. They were eventually joined by boat-building people making the long, dangerous journey from the Pacific islands.

Wherever America's new people settled, they changed their ways to suit their new home. By the time it was discovered by the rest of the world, America's various people had developed hundreds of languages and amazing cultures with beautiful art and music played on drums, trumpets, rattles, pipes, and flutes. Native American people watched the stars, developed farms so sophisticated that even today we still don't understand how they worked, built great monuments, and told stories of gods and ancestors.

Eventually, however, their lives would change forever. The Europeans were coming.

Thousands of miles away in the south, civilizations grew. The Aztecs built cities decorated in gold. Towers were built for astronomers and great pyramids touched the sky.

AZTECS

NOMADS

HAIDA

Native American people who lived along the West Coast (in what we now call British Columbia, Canada) called themselves Haida and carved great totem poles with animal and ancestor symbols, as well as canoes.

Some nomadic Native American tribes in North America farmed, made beautiful pottery, and lived in "pueblo" houses made from packed earth, called "adobe," which sheltered them from the sun.

INUIT

There were many different Native American tribes and groups. In the north the Inuit people made their homes from packed snow and stitched warm furs together to make clothes.

# A WHOLE NEW WORLD

Many schools still teach children that America was discovered by Christopher Columbus in 1492 when, in fact, Vikings sailed their small longboats to America 500 years before Columbus ever got there. The Vikings called this place Vinland because they found wild berries and grapes there, which could be used for making wine. Later, medieval fishermen from Britain and Portugal sailed across the Atlantic, too, catching cod along the coast, but they were just fishermen and not grand explorers, so no one took much notice of their stories of a new land across the ocean. It's thought that Columbus heard these rumors before he set off in his own ships.

Columbus never actually set foot on the American mainland but visited the islands of Cuba and Hispaniola (he thought these lands must be close to India, which is why people called Native American people "Indians"). There, he noticed the natives wore valuable gold jewelry and used primitive weapons. They would, he noted, be easy to conquer and might make good slaves.

News of Columbus's return quickly spread around Europe, with exaggerated reports that it was a land of treasure. In 1497, King Henry VII of England sent the Italian John Cabot to map the coast of North America while Columbus made more trips and Spain began sending settlers to South America. The race to conquer the New World had begun. For thousands of years Native American people had the continent to themselves—but those days were over.

Columbus always thought he had discovered a distant part of India or China. The first person to realize that America was a whole new continent was the explorer Amerigo Vespucci, who sailed there in 1497. Vespucci's tales of his trips became popular and when the mapmaker Martin Waldseemüller made his first chart of this strange new land, he called it America after Amerigo Vespucci. The name stuck.

Spain's lust for gold destroyed ways of life that had lasted thousands of years. Many Native American people died as Spain tightened its grip on its new land, plundering as much treasure as it could fit on boats and heading back across the Atlantic.

Columbus made four voyages across the Atlantic and was made governor of Spain's first colony there. The Europeans were horribly cruel to the natives.

Columbus's first voyage to America took five weeks. The first thing he did on arrival was to step ashore and claim the land as part of Spain.

In 1624, Dutch colonists bought the island of Manhattan from Native American people for a few trinkets and created a trading post. The town that grew was renamed New York after it was captured by the English in 1664.

A few old Dutch buildings can still be found there, while the famous Wall Street was built on the site of the wall that once encircled the little colony.

# EUROPEANS IN AMERICA

One of the most famous voyages in history was the journey of a small ship called the *Mayflower*, which took 102 passengers from Britain to their new home in Massachusetts, in North America in 1620. The people aboard were called Puritans and, like so many other people in history, they were looking for a home where they could practice their religion freely. Although the Puritans were not the first to settle in the New World, their journey to find freedom has become a symbol of America, a place which became known as the Land of the Free.

Back in the 15th century discovering a new continent was like discovering a new planet. Across Europe, people were fascinated by tales of the New World and, from the moment Columbus announced he had discovered America, Europeans began to settle there. In the following years, people poured into the new continent. They could have lived in peace, learning and sharing with the people they found there but instead, many chose to steal and destroy the land. For the Native American people it was a tragedy. Millions died from new European diseases they had never experienced before or were killed in battle by greedy newcomers.

Spain wasn't the only country to send new settlers. The Portuguese claimed the area that is now Brazil. Further to the north —in today's USA and Canada—Britain, Holland, Sweden, France, and Russia also built colonies. Some peaceful Native American tribes helped the new arrivals, and even saved them from starvation, but it made no difference. Just like in other areas, they died from the diseases brought over by the settlers or were violently forced from the lands of their ancestors.

As it became more European, America changed forever and so too did Europe. Ships loaded with South American gold sailed across the Atlantic and new American goods like chocolate and tobacco became popular in Europe. The Native American people had lost their home for good and it was clear that now America's future would be decided by the newcomers.

ALASKA

GREENLAND

RUPERT'S LAND

NEWFOUNDLAND

NEW FRANCE

**NORTH AMERICA**

LOUISIANA

FRENCH

SPANISH

PORTUGUESE

RUSSIAN

DUTCH

DANISH

ENGLISH

NEW
SPAIN

From the 16th
to the 19th century, areas
of North and South America
belonged to France. Today, places
like New Orleans and Baton
Rouge have French names, and a
version of French called
Quebecois is spoken
across Canada.

ATLANTIC OCEAN

NEW
GRANADA

# AMERICAN LANGUAGE

PERU

**SOUTH AMERICA**

BRAZIL

After the first Europeans traveled to the New
World hundreds of years passed before the
continents of North and South America settled
into the countries we know today. For many
years Britain, France, Spain, Russia, Portugal,
Germany, and the Netherlands divided America
up, and European languages were spoken across
the continent. However, over time, wars were
fought, treaties were made and slowly, modern
America took shape. But the languages of
those early years are still spoken across modern
America today.

LA PLATA

The Amish are
a religious group who
came from Switzerland
in the early 19th century and
settled in Pennsylvania. There
are more than 200,000 Amish
living there now who live
simple lives without
modern inventions
like cars.

84

FRENCH AMERICA

AMERICAN GERMAN

Germany sent thousands of settlers to the New World and the areas they settled still have a strong German flavor today! More than a million Americans in places like North Dakota still speak some German.

THE AMISH

SPANISH AMERICA

Hundreds of places where Spanish people settled, such as San Francisco and Los Angeles, have Spanish names and styles of architecture. Around 500 million people in both North and South America still speak Spanish.

# SLAVERY IN AMERICA

In 1955 Claudette Colvin (above) was arrested for not giving her bus seat to a white woman. Thanks to the courage of Black Americans like her, the Civil Rights movement has made great changes. In 1992, Mae Jemison (below) became the first African American woman to go into space.

Most people make incredible journeys to find better lives for themselves and their families. Sometimes, however, people are given no choice in where they move to and America's history is peppered with these stories. Between 1525 and 1865 more than 12 million Africans were forced from their homes and into slavery in America. Chained and crammed into ships, they were carried across the Atlantic Ocean away from their homes. Many died during the voyage and those who survived were sold at slave markets across the New World.

African slaves built the fortunes of their European masters. Often punished harshly for the smallest offence, they worked long hours at the worst jobs for no wages and lived in dreadful conditions. They weren't allowed any education, small children were often taken from their parents and sold, and they had no rights whatsoever.

Slavery was finally abolished in the United States in 1865. Over the following years the children and grandchildren of slaves shaped America as much as the European settlers. They learned to read and write so stories of slavery were at last heard. They opened their own businesses or moved to cities where entire neighborhoods filled with new families. African American music was so good that white people soon began to copy it. African American women, working on the maths of space flight, helped put a man on the moon. African Americans also became powerful politicians, great sporting heroes, famous actors, and wealthy businesspeople. Today, across America, the struggle for equality goes on.

Frederick Douglass (above) was an escaped slave who became the leader of the campaign to abolish slavery. The efforts of many meant that in 2009 Barack Obama (below) could rise to become the first-ever African American President of the United States.

In 1861, the United States went to war over slavery, with the free northern states fighting the slave-owning states in the south. The north won and in 1865 a law was passed freeing every slave in the United States.

Very few people knew the location of all the stations along the Underground Railroad, so if one part of the route was discovered the people there wouldn't be able to tell where the other stations were.

Many Canadian towns started as settlements where escaped slaves could earn a living, including places like Anderdon, Gambia, and New Canaan. Today, some of these have become historic sites.

# THE
# UNDERGROUND RAILROAD

Many slaves risked their lives by trying to escape being someone's property. The punishments for anyone caught doing this were brutal but many slaves preferred to take the risk rather than remain in appalling conditions. They fled to Mexico, where slavery had been abolished, or to Canada or free states in the north of the United States. By the end of the 18th century, a network had grown across the United States to help them find freedom.

Organized by white people known as Abolitionists, free African Americans, escaped slaves, and Native American people, the network was called the Underground Railroad. It wasn't an actual railroad with trains but a system of safe places, known as "stations," where escaping slaves could find food and help along the road to the next station. The location of safe houses was passed by word of mouth, and only to people who could be trusted. Punishments for helping slaves escape were harsh, but despite this the Underground Railroad spread across the United States. By 1850, it had helped around 100,000 people flee their "owners" and find a new life.

The journey was difficult. Those escaping had to cross hundreds of miles with slave catchers constantly searching for them and newspapers were full of notices offering rewards for their capture. Escaping slaves often made journeys from station to station on foot, zigzagging to help confuse anyone chasing them. Those who made it though could at last live as free men and women, and many small towns of escaped slaves grew in Canada.

Most escaping slaves were men. Women were rarely allowed to leave their masters' property and African American women traveling the roads were much more likely to attract attention. One of the few women to use the Underground Railroad, however, was Harriet Tubman (below), who made 13 more dangerous journeys to help other slaves escape. She later became famous for demanding the right to vote for all women, whatever their color or background.

The music made by African American slaves is an amazing example of how new arrivals to different countries can eventually change an entire culture. With no instruments except their own voices they created songs that had never been heard before and which evolved and inspired music that would eventually be listened to and performed around the entire globe. From rap and hip-hop to Latin music, rhythm and blues, rock, and pop music, almost all the music you might listen to today can trace its history back to African American slaves who had nothing to call their own except their songs.

African slaves passed long days working in the fields singing hymns or songs that told their stories of loss and hardship. They used the rhythms remembered from their homes in Africa and this kind of music later became known as "gospel."

African beats inspired a new kind of music called ragtime. It was easier to dance to than the blues and became popular across the nation before turning into jazz, with more complicated beats and rhythms.

GOSPEL

# AFRICAN AMERICAN MUSIC

BLUES

The sad work-songs slaves sang to each other in the fields also developed into a new form of music called "blues." Mixed with just a little influence from European folk, blues songs became very popular after the slaves were freed.

ROCK 'N' ROLL

Mixing jazz, blues, gospel, and European folk music produced thrilling rock 'n' roll in the 1940s and 1950s. Early African American rock 'n' roll pioneers like Chuck Berry were soon copied by white musicians like Elvis Presley.

# THE WEST

At the beginning of the 19th century almost everyone in the United States of America lived along the East Coast, although Spanish settlers had made the ocean voyage to settle in California on the West Coast. The middle of North America was a vast wilderness, home to Native American people and great herds of bison. In 1803, President Thomas Jefferson gave two explorers called Meriwether Lewis and William Clark the task of mapping a route across the United States.

Later named the Oregon Trail, because it stretched all the way to the state of Oregon on the Pacific coast, their path opened up another great journey: the overland voyage to the West. At first, it was only used by a few fur trappers

The Oregon Trail stretched over 2,100 miles across North America, from the city of Independence, Missouri, to Oregon City. Between 1836 and 1869 around 400,000 settlers made the long journey to find new lives in the American West.

OREGON CITY

UNITED STA

OREGON COUNTRY

FORT BRIDGER

MEXICAN TERRITORY

The journey was dangerous and many wagons got lost or stuck. Settlers often banded together for safety, forming long wagon trains. One of the first was made up of around 1,000 people and was called the "Wagon Train of 1843."

The California Gold Rush began on January 24, 1848, when gold was found at a place called Sutter's Mill. Over the next few years, California transformed into a rich state with many new towns, roads, schools, and churches.

UNORGANIZED TERRITORY

AMERICA

NDEPENDENCE

RGANIZED RRITORY

and traders. However, by 1936, wagons carrying adventurous settlers seeking lands and fortunes had begun taking the long and dangerous trip. Farmers, miners, and business owners went west and slowly, the middle of America began to change. Small towns, farms, and cattle ranches began springing up in the wilderness and Native American people were violently pushed out as the new settlers took over.

In 1848, the trickle of people exploring this new land turned into a flood when gold was discovered in California. Gripped by gold fever, hundreds of thousands of men traveled across the US to make their fortunes. Once again, Native American people were forced off their land to make room for the gold hunters. San Francisco, which had just 200 residents in 1846, became a city of 36,000 just six years later. California had become a golden state where fortunes could be made!

# CHINATOWN

In 1848 there were only a few hundred Chinese people living in America, mostly sailors and merchants. However, in 1850 a great civil war known as the Taiping Rebellion broke out in China. Thousands fled the fighting and the starvation that followed, heading across the Pacific Ocean to Gold Rush California where they might find a new life of freedom and wealth.

But instead, they found racism, distrust, and oppression. Not many people would employ the new Chinese immigrants and in order to survive they had to take the hardest, most backbreaking jobs for the lowest wages. Plantations that had once had slaves now used cheap Chinese workers. Laws were passed to stop Chinese people marrying white people and they weren't allowed to become citizens of the United States. In 1882, the US made its first and only law to stop immigration from a foreign land: China. For the next sixty years they were forbidden from making their home in America. The Chinese already in America couldn't even bring their families to join them.

Because no one had wanted to employ them the Chinese opened their own businesses. As the years passed they became successful. Today, there are millions of Americans with Chinese heritage and their culture and history have become part of the story of the United States of America. The Chinatown areas where Chinese people were forced to live were originally very poor places but over time, they often grew into colorful neighborhoods bursting with Chinese culture and sizzling flavors. White Americans began flocking to Chinatowns and today, Chinatowns across the US attract millions of tourists.

The Chinese helped build modern America. Working in all weathers, around 20,000 Chinese men completed the hardest work on America's great Transcontinental Railroad, which at last connected the East Coast to the West Coast. Many died in explosions or from accidents or disease but the engineering marvel they built changed America forever. For the first time goods and people could cross from one side of the continent to the other without the need for long wagon journeys.

Chinatown in San Francisco is the oldest in the United States and has the largest Chinese community anywhere outside Asia. Its roots stretch all the way back to the first Chinese settlers arriving in America.

Many arrivals were treated badly. Employers offered low wages, and many suffered from poverty and prejudice. Even so, these arrivals brought vibrant new life across the US, helping it become the successful and diverse place it is today.

Ellis Island grew into a massive complex of buildings with its own library, kitchens, bakeries, workshops, and dormitories where people could sleep. Today it is a museum, which still welcomes thousands of visitors every day.

JULY IV

# GIVE ME YOUR POOR

Nothing symbolizes the hope of American freedom as much as the Statue of Liberty. The huge statue was a gift from France in 1886 to honor the American hope of freedom and democracy as well as the end of slavery. At its base is a plaque with the words of a poem called "The New Colossus," which contains the line, *"Give me your tired, your poor, your huddled masses yearning to breathe free."* The statue was an invitation from America to the people of the world and millions accepted.

The people of the world arrived at a huge immigration center on Ellis Island. Boatloads of arrivals came ashore almost every day and were treated politely. Each arrival was given a medical test and asked a few questions before being allowed to enter New York City. However, until the mid-20th century, Chinese and Asian people, gay people, and anyone with a disease or disability were banned from entering the country. But between 1836 and 1914 the United States took in the greatest wave of immigrants the world has ever seen. More than 30 million boarded ships, escaping poverty or oppression in their own homelands and in 1907 alone 1,285,349 immigrants entered America through Ellis Island.

They came mostly from Europe and Russia: poor, unskilled workers, families with all their belongings in a suitcase or two, professors, architects, artists, musicians, and every other type of person imaginable. It was the greatest movement of people the world had ever seen and not only did many achieve their dreams of a new life but the arrivals changed the face of America forever. Millions of people building better lives for themselves meant new art, inventions, stores, and businesses. Those who made the journey found that the Statue of Liberty filled her promise and over the years all those different people became one people: Americans.

The Statue of Liberty was designed by Frédéric Auguste Bartholdi and is a statue of the Roman goddess of freedom, Libertas. In her right hand she holds a torch, bringing light to the world and, beneath her feet, half-hidden by her robes, is a broken chain that symbolized the end of slavery in the United States.

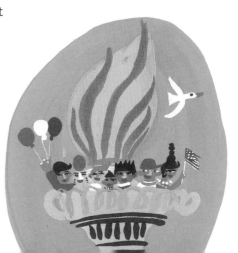

The Germans arrived in America in the days when there were only a handful of people living in small colonies on the East Coast. Their numbers grew in the 19th century and millions of Germans helped build modern America. The German engineer John Roebling designed New York City's famous Brooklyn Bridge while German immigrants introduced America to the hot dog and to traditions such as decorating trees at Christmastime. Levi Strauss arrived in the United States in 1847 and six years later began building a company that made the world's first jeans!

GERMANS

RUSSIANS

In the 19th and early 20th century millions of Russians headed to New York and Ellis Island. Many were poor farmers, but the more well-to-do came as well—often Jewish people suffering oppression in Russia. They brought their culture with them: classical music and ballet as well as literature, fashion, and acting. Many Russian immigrants were scientists who helped the United States become world-leaders in science, teaching their knowledge to students in American universities. Today the descendants of Russian immigrants are among some of the greatest names in American sports, music, movies, and writing.

ITALIANS

# AMERICA'S NEW PEOPLE

Millions of people from across Europe and beyond journeyed to the United States in answer to the Statue of Liberty's call for the tired and the poor. Many were escaping oppression or poverty and each different group brought with them the flavors of their home country.

IRISH

The Irish were among the first settlers of the New World—when a great famine struck Ireland in 1845, many thousands escaped starvation by traveling to the United States. Over time they would go on to make a huge impact as politicians, journalists, and sportspeople, especially in cities like New York, Boston, and Chicago. Even today, Chicago dyes its river green on St Patrick's Day, in honor of Ireland's national saint. Great Irish Americans have included John F. Kennedy, one of the United States' most-loved presidents.

In the 18th and 19th centuries parts of Italy suffered terrible poverty that left people starving. Many families left everything behind to start a new life in America. There, they changed America in many ways. The US fell in love with the food the Italians brought with them. The children of Italian immigrants were also among the first to take African American jazz music and, with the help of Eastern European Jewish songwriters, turn it into a completely new sound with an Italian influence. Singers with Italian parents, like Frank Sinatra, gave the US a new kind of pop music.

# GHETTOS

The word "ghetto" was first used in 16th-century Venice, in Italy, and originally described a poor part of the city where Jewish people lived. "Ghetto" is sometimes used to mean an area within a city where many people with the same background or nationality live. If we look back to Brick Lane, it could be described as a ghetto, where the first Huguenots lived, then Jewish folk, and now Bengalis. Over time, as new communities settle in their adopted land (and make more money) they usually move on to new homes in different places, mingling with the wider population.

Often, immigrants arriving in new countries were poor. They had to take the worst jobs with little pay and couldn't afford to live in richer areas. The only places they could afford to live were slums

Harlem, in New York City, was one of the country's most famous ghettos. In the early 20th century Harlem became a center of African American culture with its own stores, schools, and the famous Apollo Theater.

Many Jewish immigrants from eastern Europe made their home in New York's Lower East Side. Many songwriters, movie-makers and theater stars began their careers here.

where large families were crammed into small apartments. Moving to a new land where you don't have a job or know anyone is also scary, and most new arrivals found it comforting to find places to live where their neighbors spoke the same language. Sometimes these immigrants were forced to live in the same area, as was the case in Chinatown in San Francisco.

With so many immigrants arriving, the United States had ghettos in every city. Here people who had once been slaves lived, or new arrivals from Italy or Russia or Ireland set up their homes. Today, many of these areas are vibrant and colorful historic areas where visitors can still find the sights, sounds, and flavors of different parts of the world.

# THE MOVEMENT OF IDEAS

By 1933 the Nazis had already started making laws forbidding Jewish people from holding any public office or teaching in universities. Germany's loss was America's gain as the great scientist Albert Einstein (above) traveled to the US and went through Ellis Island like any other new immigrant.

In 1884, an inventor from Serbia by the name of Nikola Tesla (below) moved to New York where his ideas about electrical currents helped create the modern world, where electricity can be used in homes.

For people of color—especially for the descendants of slaves and Chinese settlers—the United States could be a cruel and brutal place. But for white immigrants from Europe it was a different story. Although most started their new lives poor, doing the worst jobs for little money, for Europeans the United States during the 19th and 20th centuries was a place where talent could eventually shine. Many who had been hungry, mistreated, or bullied in their own countries decided to take their chances in America. They came for different reasons but had one goal in common: to find a better life for themselves and their families.

The United States was a huge, exciting country looking toward the future. It was hungry for new businesses, fashions, and entertainment. In 1893 and 1904 the United States invited inventors, architects, engineers, performers, musicians, and artists from around the globe to spectacular World Fairs where their breathtaking ideas and designs were seen by millions.

Fashion designers, moviemakers, scientists, writers, and entertainers all made the journey to this promising new land. Many arrived with little money and few belongings, but with hard work and ambition they and their children achieved success they could never have dreamed of in their home countries. Throughout the 19th and 20th centuries America led the world in new inventions and entertainments; with the help of European engineers, electricity arrived in many homes; many Hollywood movies made by and starring immigrants were seen around the world; fabulous restaurants were opened by immigrants; European architects changed city skylines across the nation; and new American music, written by immigrants, made the world dance and sing. Thanks to its immigrants, the United States became a place where dreams could come true.

Charlie Chaplin (above) was born in the slums of London and became an entertainer to earn money. Age nineteen, he left Britain and headed to Hollywood where he became one of the most famous people in the world, writing, directing, and acting in internationally successful movies.

The oppression of races and religions continues. Sergey Brin (below) left Russia with his Jewish family because of persecution in 1979. Russia should have made an effort to keep the brilliant young man because he went on to co-found Google!

Architecture is an amazing example of how immigration helped shape America. Today, the country is famous for tall skyscrapers but the ideas that shaped these ultra-modern buildings started in Germany. The German Nazis hated the originality coming out of the small Bauhaus school of architecture. It was forced to close and many of its architects fled to the US where they helped define the country's buildings, designing bold, simple homes and stunning block-like skyscrapers. These ideas were widely copied, making the United States the most modern, futuristic-looking country in the world.

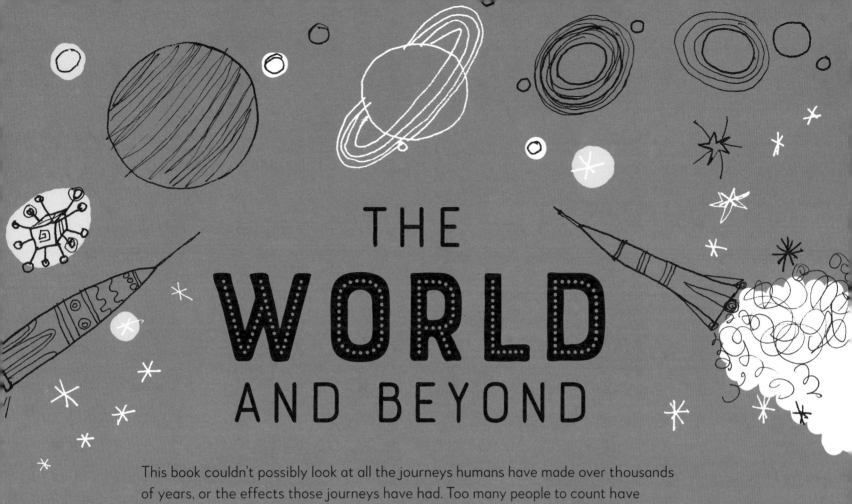

# THE WORLD
## AND BEYOND

This book couldn't possibly look at all the journeys humans have made over thousands of years, or the effects those journeys have had. Too many people to count have traveled to new homes, and every single one of those journeys has made the world a different place. Great movements of people have changed history in amazing ways.

It's worth remembering that every mass movement is made up of lots of individual people. Even those who don't come up with a world-changing invention or become famous still make a difference to their new community. One person settling in a new place will bring their own stories and their own ideas, as well as their own food, music, heritage, or culture. Just one single person can make a difference to an entire community—their arrival makes ripples that spread for years.

This is how the modern world was made: by people swapping ideas. When we close our minds and our hearts to others, we close the door on progress. For example, when Brick Lane welcomed the Huguenots, Britain opened its arms to skills that benefited the whole country. When people meet as friends, we move forward together.

The most famous journeys that have helped shape our world fill the pages of this book: tales of war, poverty, and oppression that have forced people to move, and people whose journeys have helped make history. But there is still more to look at and understand. Immigration can take lots of different forms—even birds and animals make journeys! We'll also find out what happens when everyday people make a journey to a new country and look at some of the stranger places where they have traveled. Plus, we'll discover journeys going on right now and even into the far future. Perhaps the next great human journey will be to a completely new planet!

# GREAT JOURNEYS OF THE
## ANIMAL WORLD

The journey of the wildebeest is one of the most impressive sights in the animal kingdom. They gather in herds of more than one million to protect themselves from lions and crocodiles as they travel between Kenya and Tanzania in search of fresh grass to eat.

Some people make adventurous journeys because they are curious to see the world. Others move to escape poverty or war. But almost everyone who migrates does so to seek a better life for themselves and their family.

Humans aren't the only species to do this. Around the world, birds, mammals, reptiles, and even insects make amazing journeys every year. They are looking for more food and warmer climates where they can raise their young. Some travel short distances, but others make incredibly long journeys round the world, chasing warmer weather and plentiful food.

The Monarch Butterfly can't survive the cold winters of the northern United States. So every year, these beautiful insects flap up to 3,000 miles in great swarms to California and Mexico where the weather is warmer.

For example, every year the Arctic tern flies all the way from the Arctic, at the top of the Earth, to Antarctica, at the bottom, and back. Its wings carry it on a journey of over 20,000 miles! Many birds, whales, fish, insects, and other animals travel to places over thousands of miles away. Animals have incredible navigation skills, using the sun, stars, and moon to guide them over long distances.

So when you next see birds flying south for the winter, remember that the world is full of amazing journeys, and we humans aren't so different to the animals all around us.

Every year the Arctic tern sees TWO summers! It travels from the Arctic in the far north, to feed in the Antarctic summer on the other side of the world in the distant south. It flies all the way back six months later.

Tens of thousands of years ago, giant animals known as megafauna roamed the Earth: elephants much bigger than those we see today, armadillos as big as cars, and many more. No one knows exactly why they died out but in many cases it seems to have happened soon after humans moved into the area. Even as recently as 250 years ago species on the Commander Islands became extinct when humans settled there. It seems that since the beginning of our history, humans have hunted many animals to extinction.

# THE TROUBLE WITH HUMANS

Today, we often think of animal extinctions—when whole species are wiped out—as a recent problem caused by cutting down forests and over-hunting, but it's something that has happened for as long as there have been humans. Throughout history, when humans journeyed to new places, they often destroyed the animal and plant life that was already there.

For thousands of years, Native American peoples hunted buffalo (also known as bison) across the great plains of America, only killing what they needed for their meat and skins. But as the United States opened up in the mid-19th century (especially after the construction of the railways) new hunters arrived. Armed with guns rather than bows and spears, the new arrivals shot the buffalo not for food but for sport. One man alone— a hunter called Orlando Brown—killed 6,000 of them. By 1880 the number of buffalo had fallen from around 30 million to just 1,000.

The challenge for all of us today is to learn that as well as respecting each other, we must learn to respect nature and the fantastic creatures we share Earth with. Around the world efforts are being made to stop people hunting and killing endangered species, and to protect natural environments so that rare animals can live in peace. Thanks to this the numbers of some animals—like mountain gorillas, grey whales, and giraffes—are increasing, but others are still in danger and many need our help if they are to survive.

109

Also known simply as "the plague," the Black Death was one of the worst outbreaks of disease in history. Because it spread a long time ago—in the mid-14th century—we are unsure of how many people were infected, but it is thought that as many as 200 million people across Asia, Europe, and Africa may have died of the disease. Today, researchers believe that it started in central Asia, traveling along the Silk Road to Europe. From there, it infected fleas on the rats on merchant ships that sailed around the Mediterranean Sea and beyond.

THE BLACK DEATH
14TH CENTURY

# THE JOURNEYS OF DISEASES

The more that humans have traveled, the more that deadly diseases have been carried from one place to another. For example, when Europeans arrived in America they brought new diseases that Native American people had never seen before. Because they had no natural immunity, like the Europeans, they died in their thousands. Throughout history, this is something that has occurred again and again.

THE FLU PANDEMIC 1918

A pandemic happens when a disease spreads around the whole world, and the flu outbreak of 1918 did exactly that. At the end of World War I, millions of soldiers were gathered in large groups in Europe, either in hospitals or in large camps waiting to go home. The flu spread quickly among them and when the soldiers returned to their homes around the world, they took the sickness with them. Eventually, around 500 million—a third of the world's people—caught the flu and anywhere between 20 and 50 million people died before the sickness died out, two years after it first appeared, in 1920.

In December 2019, a new virus called Covid-19 or "Coronavirus" broke out in China. A few weeks later, cases were being reported in many countries. As a result, flights were grounded, travel was stopped around the world, and by March 2020, it was declared to be a pandemic. Around the world, people were forced to stay inside or wear masks if they had to go outside. In one of the great scientific achievements of history, a vaccine was created late in 2020. That meant the world could begin the fight against the deadly disease.

# THE CORONAVIRUS
## 2019

POLONEZKÖY

In Turkey there is a village called Polonezköy. The name means "Polish village" and it was settled in 1842 by a handful of people from Poland. It still has connections with Polish culture today.

WELSH PATAGONIA

Over 8,000 miles away from Wales is the country of Patagonia where between 1,500 and 5,000 people speak Welsh! In the 19th century their ancestors journeyed to a place where they could create a Wales of their own.

In the 1970s Vietnam was devastated by war. Hundreds of thousands of people fled by boat but many died at sea during the long, dangerous journeys. Refugee camps sprang up in places a long, long way from Vietnam.

In the early 20th century, Japanese people fleeing poverty headed to Brazil, where they worked on coffee plantations. Today, around two million Brazilians have Japanese heritage.

# STRANGE MIGRATIONS

We've looked at some of the most famous movements of people, from the first steps of hunter-gatherers in Africa to millions of people arriving in modern America. But people have made other journeys that can seem quite unexpected, moving from one part of the world to strange, faraway places...

## THE IRISH HERMITS OF ICELAND

Iceland was discovered and populated by Vikings around 1,000 years ago—but they weren't the only new arrivals. Monks from Ireland—called Papar—made the dangerous voyage to Iceland where they lived as hermits, devoting themselves to Christianity, all alone and far away from other people.

Many of the things we eat every day are the result of people traveling. Chocolate, for example, was thought to be a gift from the gods by the Aztecs in ancient South America before it was brought to Europe in the 16th century.

# THE
# UNEXPECTED
# CONSEQUENCES
## OF TRAVEL

When people move around the world, they carry with them original ideas, flavors, sounds, styles, and different ways of living. There are thousands of unexpected ways in which human journeys around the world have changed communities.

Take a look around and you might start to see examples that you walk past every day without ever noticing before: Islamic mosques, Jewish synagogues, or Hindu temples. You might see festivals like Eid or Diwali when people from different parts of the world celebrate their traditions. Try counting all the different businesses that might not be there if we humans didn't travel so much: restaurants serving Indian, Thai, or Turkish food. In some cities Australian travelers have opened Australian pubs, or you might see stores and market stalls selling foods and spices from the Caribbean. Wherever you live it's likely you'll find signs of human journeys from around the globe.

Examples of how human journeys and migration have changed our world are all around us. More than ever, the human race is mixed together in all sorts of ways that we hardly ever notice. It's hard to imagine now how different life might be without all the wonderful things that human journeys have brought us. However, one thing is for sure: it would be a lot more boring!

When you're brushing your teeth, you're using an invention from China that traveled to Europe along the Silk Road in the 15th century. The first toothbrushes had bamboo or bone handles and the brushes were made with bristles from pig skin!

115

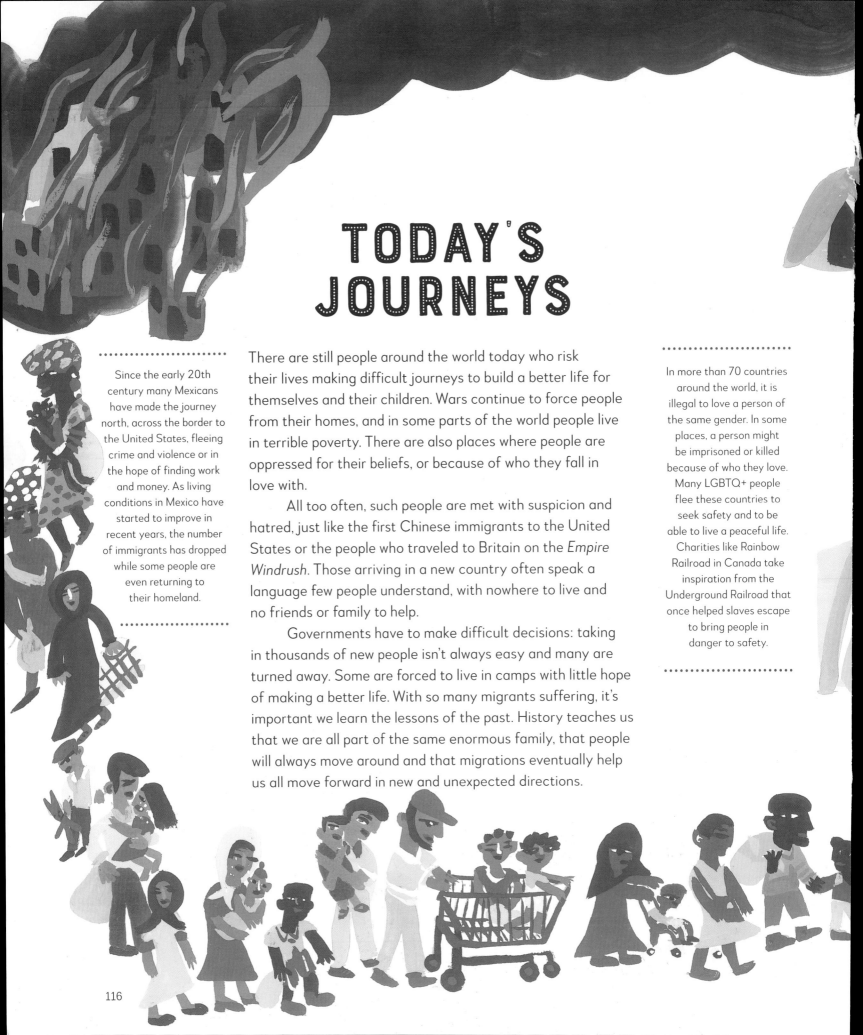

# TODAY'S JOURNEYS

Since the early 20th century many Mexicans have made the journey north, across the border to the United States, fleeing crime and violence or in the hope of finding work and money. As living conditions in Mexico have started to improve in recent years, the number of immigrants has dropped while some people are even returning to their homeland.

There are still people around the world today who risk their lives making difficult journeys to build a better life for themselves and their children. Wars continue to force people from their homes, and in some parts of the world people live in terrible poverty. There are also places where people are oppressed for their beliefs, or because of who they fall in love with.

All too often, such people are met with suspicion and hatred, just like the first Chinese immigrants to the United States or the people who traveled to Britain on the *Empire Windrush*. Those arriving in a new country often speak a language few people understand, with nowhere to live and no friends or family to help.

Governments have to make difficult decisions: taking in thousands of new people isn't always easy and many are turned away. Some are forced to live in camps with little hope of making a better life. With so many migrants suffering, it's important we learn the lessons of the past. History teaches us that we are all part of the same enormous family, that people will always move around and that migrations eventually help us all move forward in new and unexpected directions.

In more than 70 countries around the world, it is illegal to love a person of the same gender. In some places, a person might be imprisoned or killed because of who they love. Many LGBTQ+ people flee these countries to seek safety and to be able to live a peaceful life. Charities like Rainbow Railroad in Canada take inspiration from the Underground Railroad that once helped slaves escape to bring people in danger to safety.

More than 13.5 million people have fled Syria to escape a terrible civil war. Hundreds of thousands have journeyed over land on foot, while others try and reach other countries in unsafe boats.

The Syrians' story is a sad one. Many have died along the way. Many are still in camps, waiting for help to come. Although a few have found the better life they were seeking, too many lives have been ruined by the war.

# CLIMATE CHANGE
## MIGRATION

In coastal parts of the United States, rising ocean levels are already causing people to move to higher ground. In some places, whole communities like the people of Isle de Jean Charles in Louisiana have had to move.

We've seen how in Africa, climate change transformed green lands into deserts and forced people to move to places where they could find water. Today climate change is still with us, but has been made worse by pollution and environmental damage caused by humans. Rivers are drying up. The ice caps in the Arctic and Antarctica are melting, causing ocean levels to rise, flooding islands and coastal communities. The weather has changed, too. Devastating storms and higher rainfall have caused floods and destroyed homes.

The number of people forced to move because of climate change is steadily increasing. So far, millions have already been affected and some researchers say that by 2050, as many as a billion people will have to leave their homes, creating the largest movement of people in history.

But the story isn't over yet. People are starting to realize what a terrible catastrophe climate change is for life on Earth and are working to slow it down. Scientists, researchers, and ordinary people are working to find ways to make sure the future of our planet is as bright as possible.

In Africa, countries are under threat of being swallowed by the growing Sahara Desert. People are working together on the Great Green Wall, which will grow billions of trees and plants across the entire width of Africa to stop the desert growing.

New ways of farming such as vertical farming and deep farming in old mines are being explored, so that farmland can be returned to nature.

Today, people around the world are working to stop the worst effects of climate change and prevent people losing their homes. Countries around the world are slowly changing to green energy, like solar power.

119

# THE NEXT
# GREAT HUMAN JOURNEY

Today, there are more humans in the world than ever before. Eve—the woman who left Africa 70,000 years ago—now has nearly eight billion great-great-great-(add a LOT more "greats")-grandchildren. With new inventions in farming and housing —and by sharing what we have—humans will live on Earth for many thousands of years to come, but we are now turning our attention to space. We have landed on the moon and sent people to live on space stations but, for a long time, scientists have wondered if humans could ever live on a new planet permanently. Today, they are working toward that goal. The planet they have chosen is Mars. You may be able to see it from your bedroom window on a clear night.

Building a colony on a new planet will be expensive and difficult. Mars is a long, long way away. There is no oxygen there, or life of any sort. It's extremely cold. The soil is toxic, so there's no food. Without the protection of special space suits and oxygen tanks to breathe, humans would die on Mars. But people have always made dangerous journeys of discovery, and made new homes in the wilderness. Today, space agencies like NASA, as well as businesses, are making plans to start a permanent colony on Mars. It is very possible that within your lifetime you will see the next great human journey; the most amazing step forward in human evolution. Perhaps you might even travel to Mars yourself!

Living on Mars might sound like something from a science-fiction movie but companies like SpaceX are already developing the technology needed. Their plan is to put humans on Mars by 2024.

Mars is very different to Earth, but of all the planets in the Solar System, it is the most similar to our own. It has water, days just a little longer than Earth's 24 hours, and seasons—though a year on Mars lasts 687 days!

One of the ways we might make life possible is called "terraforming." This would take hundreds of years. Humans would at first live underground, protected from the Martian environment, while they slowly worked to change an entire planet.

An atmosphere would be created for Mars to make it warmer. Specially adapted microbes might make the soil suitable for plants, which would start making oxygen. In the distant future, Mars might even have lakes and forests, just like Earth.

Cuba once had a close relationship with the United States. But in the 1950s, it changed its government with a violent revolution. Ties with the US were cut, and trade was banned. Cuba became much more isolated.

Thousands of Cubans fled the country, often in small boats headed for Florida. In Cuba, no new ideas or private businesses were allowed. Few people arrived from abroad. For decades very little changed.

# NO IMMIGRATION

In the Bay of Bengal, east of India, is an island known as North Sentinel Island, where a group of hunter-gatherers live. Almost nothing is known about these people because—in the past, they have attacked anyone attempting to make contact, even firing arrows at helicopters. Today, no one is allowed near the island and these ancient folk have been left to live as their ancestors lived.

What would happen if it was decided that people weren't allowed to make journeys? Throughout history there have been very few places that didn't allow new people in but studying them can help give us an idea of what our world might look like if we did not live in a world full of journeys.

A famous example is Japan's 220-year lockdown. From 1633 to 1853, the country shut its borders almost completely. To stop the spread of Western ideas and Christianity, Japan allowed only a few merchant ships to sail into special ports. For Japanese people, leaving the country was forbidden. During this time, the West started an Industrial Revolution, invented long-distance communication with the "telegraph," and built great steam ships. When the ban was finally lifted, Japan had fallen behind the rest of the world—its culture had stayed almost exactly the same as it was in the 1600s.

This example shows us that without journeys change happens more slowly. Some people might think this is a good thing, because they think that change is bad. While it's true that change can bring problems, without journeys our world today would be very different. Since the dawn of our existence, and the first journey from Africa, we humans have made journeys to every corner of our world. We don't just live in a world full of journeys—the world has been created by those journeys.

# THE ENDLESS JOURNEY

DNA is a tiny molecule that exists within all known living things. Scientists can now study anyone's DNA and accurately see where their ancestors came from. Around the world many people are finding out that their heritage is a lot more varied and interesting than they could ever have guessed!

Inside your DNA—the building blocks in your body that make you, YOU—are marks left by your ancestors. Imagine them: a line of people stretching back thousands and thousands of years. You'd find people who lived in the same place all their lives, and some who made great journeys around the world. You might be related to Vikings and Roman soldiers, Italian merchants or Portuguese pirates, nobles of far-off countries, Roma travelers, or Huguenot refugees. Way, way back, at the beginning of your huge family tree, would be the first woman to leave Africa.

Wherever we live now, inside us all are travelers who arrived from somewhere else. The fact that you are here at all means you are part of a great migration that still goes on today. Since humans made their first journeys, people from different parts of the world have been making friends and telling their stories; sharing ideas, recipes, music, and much more. Some have fallen in love and had children. Others opened businesses or lived quietly in their new homes, working and raising families. Many have stood up for the rights of others like them and helped equality to move forward. History doesn't always remember such people, but they have all helped create a world where you were possible.

Today, the world still has problems, but those problems will never be solved with hatred and unfairness. When we look back, history teaches us that human journeys have always taken place and always will. We should celebrate those journeys because when we travel in friendship and arrive in peace, we walk together toward a world with amazing new possibilities.

Each and every one of us is here because we are part of long journeys around the world. There are traveling adventurers in all of us! Your ancestors might have been hunter-gatherers, traders, soldiers, or refugees—you might have traces of all of those from different places and times!

125

# GLOSSARY

**Abolish**  to put an end to a practice or institution

**Abolitionist**  a person who favors the end of slavery

**Apartheid**  a policy that separates groups of people based on their skin color and decides rights, relations, and privileges according to their race

**Architecture**  the art of designing and constructing buildings

**Astronomer**  a scientist who studies the stars, planets, and other natural objects in space

**Cargoes**  goods carried on a ship or some sort of transportation

**Civilization**  a complex human society, made up of different cities and cultures

**Climate Change**  the long-term alteration of temperature and typical weather patterns in an area

**Colony**  a group of people who have moved to a new area but have strong cultural ties to their home country

**Conqueror**  someone who gains ownership over a place or people (normally through force or war)

**Deep Farming**  a vertical farm built from remade underground tunnels and mine shafts

**Didgeridoo**  an Australian Aboriginal wind instrument in the form of a long wooden tube

**Diwali**  a festival of lights celebrated by Hindus, Jains, Sikhs, and some Buddhists

**DNA**  the genetic information responsible for the development and function of a living thing

**Eid**  a festival celebrated by Muslims worldwide

**Empire**  a group of countries ruled over by a single person of power

**Endangered**  a species that is of high risk of extinction

**Evolution**  the growth and development of animals and plants over time

**Extinction**  a species (animal or plant) that no longer exists because they have died out with no other members to breed with

**Globalization**  the speed up of movement and trade all over the world

**Heritage**  something that can be handed down from the past, e.g. culture, traditions, objects, etc

**Homo Sapiens**  the Latin word for human

**Immigration**  the action of moving permanently to a foreign country

**Immunity**  the ability for someone to resist an infection or disease

**Lieutenant**  a deputy or someone acting for a superior

**Longships**  a type of warship sailed by Vikings as they traveled the world

**Lyre**  a string instrument like a small U-shaped harp with strings attached to a crossbar

**Martian**  relates to inhabitants from the planet Mars

**Medieval Europe**  a time period in Europe from the 5th century to the 15th century

**Meditation**  focusing one's mind for a period of time in silence or with the aid of chanting for religious or spiritual purposes or as a method of relaxation

**Merchant**   a person who travels across lands to trade goods such as metal, weapons, or spices

**Migration**   the movement from one place to another with the intention of settling

**Mosque**   a Muslim place of worship

**Neanderthals**   an extinct species of human who lived in Europe around 35,000 years ago

**NHS**   stands for the National Health Service, which is a healthcare service everyone in the UK can use

**Nobel Peace Prize**   an award given to an individual for their work in helping to maintain peace to make their country a better place

**Nomads**   groups of people who continuously move from place to place

**Oppression**   prolonged cruelty or unjust treatment

**Pandemic**   the outbreak of an infectious disease across the whole world

**Penal Colony**   an area (often an island) used to exile prisoners and separate them from the general population

**Plantation**   an estate on which crops such as coffee, sugar, and tobacco are grown

**Pollution**   the introduction of a substance into the environment that can be harmful or poisonous

**Poverty**   the state of being extremely poor

**Prejudice**   preconceived opinion that is not based on reason or actual experience

**Primitive**   relating to an early stage in the historical development of something

**Protest**   to express your disapproval about something through written, verbal, or physical action

**Psychedelic**   art or graphics that were influenced by the hippie movement, peace, and culture in India (mainly Buddhism)

**Puritans**   a group of Christian Protestants from England who followed strict moral rules

**Racism**   prejudice and discrimination by an individual, community, or institution against a person or people based on their skin color

**Refugee**   a person who has been forced to leave their country in order to escape war, natural disaster, or persecution

**Revolution**   to overthrow a government or social order in favor of a new system

**Segregation**   the systematic action of separating people into racial or ethnic groups in daily life

**Settlement**   a place where people establish a community

**Slavery**   the condition in which one human being is owned by another

**Slums**   an overcrowded urban street or area where very poor people live

**Spanish Flamenco Dance Music**   a form of song, dance, and instrumental music commonly associated with the Roma of southern Spain

**Synagogue**   the building where Jewish people meet for religious worship

**Terraforming**   to transform another planet so that it resembles earth and humans can live there

**The British Commonwealth**   a group of nations that were once part of the British Empire

**Treaty**   a formal legally binding agreement between two countries

**Vertical Farming**   the practice of growing crops in vertical stacked layers

**West Indian**   refers to people originating from the Caribbean

To everybody who has made a journey to find a better life. It takes such courage, which should be celebrated.
This book is for you – C.C.
For my family, who journeyed with me to make a new life in a new country – M.H.

First Published in 2022 by Frances Lincoln Children's Books,
an imprint of The Quarto Group.
100 Cummings Center, Suite 265D, Beverly, MA 01915, USA.
T +1 978-282-9590 F +1 078-283-2742 www.QuartoKnows.com

A catalogue record for this book is available from the British Library.

ISBN 978-0-7112-5619-4
eISBN 978-0-7112-5620-0

The illustrations were created in gouache
Set in Woodford Bourne Pro

Published by Katie Cotton and Peter Marley
Designed by Mike Jolley
Edited by Lucy Menzies and Claire Grace
Production by Dawn Cameron

Manufactured in Singapore CO112021

1 3 5 7 9 8 6 4 2